HOW TO
SPEAK BRIT

The Quintessential Guide to
the King's English, Cockney Slang, and
Other Flummoxing British Phrases

CHRISTOPHER J. MOORE

GOTHAM BOOKS

First published in North America in 2014 by

GOTHAM BOOKS
Published by the Penguin Group
Penguin Group (USA) LLC
375 Hudson Street
New York, New York 10014

USA I Canada I UK I Ireland I Australia I New Zealand I India I South Africa I China
penguin.com
A Penguin Random House Company

Copyright © 2014 Elwin Street Productions
Elwin Street Productions
3 Percy Street
London, W1T 1DE
United Kingdom
elwinstreet.com

Library of Congress Cataloging-in-Publication Data has been applied for.
ISBN 978-1-592-40898-6

Printed in the United States of America

10 9 8 7 6 5 4 3 2 1

Illustrations: Stephen Brayda
Additional text: Anna May

Contents

Introduction

There is something that has to be understood straightaway about the British: As soon as you open your mouth, your listener puts you into a social category. "Language most shewes a man: speake that I may see thee," wrote the playwright Ben Jonson as early as 1641 to point out that your life could literally depend on the way you spoke. The principle of respecting the King's English was already well established by the mid-seventeenth century and we have to go back some two-hundred years further to find where it all started.

In the Middle Ages, Latin and French had been the languages of government and diplomacy, but during the Renaissance the change to vernacular languages was happening all over Europe, and England was no exception. As yet, English had little or no standard spelling and existed in a thousand different varieties and dialects. Only around the start of the fifteenth century did a standard form of English begin to be adopted for government business in London, thus establishing a court English as opposed to a country English. When William Caxton set up his printing press later that century, this was the standard he adopted, initiating an industry so successful that here we are, still at it, making books.

As for the actual expression, "the King's English," Thomas Wilson appears to have been the first to use it in his *Art of Rhetorique* of 1553, where he takes to task the pretensions of those who infect the English language with fancy foreign borrowings, or what he calls "strange inkhorn terms." Wilson was so irritated with what he saw as a departure from plain speech that he wrote, "they forget altogether their mother's language. And I dare swear this, if some of their mothers were alive, they were not able to tell what they say, and yet these fine English clerks will say they speak in their mother tongue, if a man should charge them for counterfeiting the King's English."

Over the next three centuries, many other writers pursued the same ideal, driven by their annoyance with lax standards to publish guides and norms for good writing and speaking. Educationalists followed suit, with the newly founded grammar schools teaching good practice.

Language was increasingly the key that opened the door to elegant society, employment, and advancement. Lessons in elocution—the art of speaking properly—became a necessary part of the education of any young lady, especially those, like Jane Austen's heroines, in search of a husband with estates and an income of more than three thousand a year.

Perhaps the most famous example in literature of the social power of *received* English is found in George Bernard Shaw's 1916 play *Pygmalion*, popularized in the 1960s stage musical and movie *My Fair Lady*. Here, Shaw complained bitterly, "It is impossible for an Englishman to open his mouth without making some other Englishman hate or despise him."

To give a flavor of Shaw's irritation, we need only turn to the opening scene of the play where Eliza Doolittle, a Cockney flower girl, encounters the mother of a young man who asks her how the girl knows her son:

ELIZA. *Ow, eez ye-ooa san, is e? Wal, fewd dan y' de-ooty bawmz*
a mather should, eed now bettern to spawl a pore gel's flahrzn
than ran awy athaht pyin. Will ye-oo py me f'them? [Shaw's note:
Here, with apologies, this desperate attempt to represent her
dialect without a phonetic alphabet must be abandoned as
unintelligible outside London.]

Eliza, painfully aware of her dreadful Cockney accent, goes
to see Henry Higgins, a professor of phonetics, to ask him for
elocution lessons. The professor, spurred on by a bet with a friend,
takes on the challenge of changing the flower girl's speech and
manners to make her acceptable to upper-class London society. In
the end, like the sculptor Pygmalion in the classical myth, he falls
in love with his own successful creation.

However, we are in another world now. From the 1940s
onwards, new linguistic theories emerged, banishing the insistence
on *correctness* that our elders used to teach us. From then on, all
varieties of language became new hunting grounds, and linguists
raced about cataloging dialects and tongues, the rarer and more
threatened the better. In the remotest corners of Britain, modest
and retiring grannies were surprised to find microphones thrust
under their noses, with the invitation to sing, chant, or narrate
anything that came into their heads.

Society and education moved rapidly with this change in
attitude. Added to the new linguistic freedoms was that of
ignorance, as grammar was no longer taught in schools, and no
British person under the age of forty now has any idea what a
substantive, preposition, or adverb is, let alone the correct use
of the apostrophe.

The BBC, slow to change but quick to keep up its listening
audience figures, showed how to move with the times in

broadcasting. Local radio DJs were recruited off the street, or from pirate radio stations, with their local accents, jokes, and rapid-fire wit. Accents became the new cachet, attractively packaged to represent real, live people rather than social constructs. Among the shifts in perception, a national bank discovered that its telephone clients seemed to trust a Scottish accent more than any other, and so it was to be.

Linguists gave us the freedom to speak as we like, and as a result, perhaps at no time since the first Elizabethan period, when Shakespeare took full advantage of it, has the language been in such a state of rapid and creative change. The sheer inventiveness of English is what captures the imagination.

It's a Dog's Life

The comforts of hearth and home are central to the British sense of well-being. A cozy, private home with a roaring fire to keep the gloomy weather at bay, a pipe and slippers, and a cherished dog snoozing at your feet—all of these are parts of the British psyche that run deep. Home may be a magnificent **manor**, a modest **semi-detached**, or a clapped out caravan, but for a Brit, there's simply no better place to be.

Aga (noun)

A heavy duty, cast-iron stove cherished by middle-class Brits as a symbol of home and its comforts.

An Aga is a rather unusual and extremely expensive kind of domestic stove, which has become an iconic piece of equipment for a certain type of British household. The Aga's inventor, Gustaf Dalén (1869–1937), was a blind, 1912 Nobel Laureate for Physics. Wanting a stove without knobs and controls and that didn't require constant tending, Dalén went about designing a self-regulating version for his own kitchen.

Agas, despite being somewhat clunky in appearance, are surprisingly fuel-efficient and capable of running for twenty-four hours on only eight pounds of solid fuel while producing an intense and lasting radiant heat.

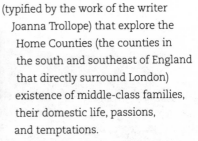

Now over eighty years old, the Aga has come under British ownership and, with its enthusiastic adoption by middle-class households, has acquired an essentially British character. It has even inspired a modern genre of novels known as *Aga-Sagas* (typified by the work of the writer Joanna Trollope) that explore the Home Counties (the counties in the south and southeast of England that directly surround London) existence of middle-class families, their domestic life, passions, and temptations.

Yet none of this tells you what exactly the appeal of an Aga is, why owners fall hopelessly in love with them, nor why their Aga appears to represent for them an ideal of home comfort and convenience. You will just have to find someone who owns one, and ask them. Make sure you allow plenty of time for the long, detailed, and enthusiastic reply.

Bloomsbury (proper noun)

A faded, yet elegant, area in central London near the British Museum, known as the home for scandalous behavior by the literary and artistic set in the early twentieth century.

Once characterized by Georgian period squares, and known for its bookshops, publishing houses, and social elegance, Bloomsbury was devastated by German bombs during the Second World War.

In the 1970s, London University and its construction of charmless, concrete buildings left the area a pale shadow of what it once was.

Yet echoes of a more elegant, if risqué, past are still present. The so-called Bloomsbury Group in London had something of the same notoriety as the literary and artistic Americans who congregated in Paris around the 1920s and scandalized everyone with their unconventional lifestyles. Future publisher Leonard Woolf, while an undergraduate at Cambridge, had already established relationships with an elite group of young intellectuals known as the *Apostles*. Later, with his wife, novelist Virginia Woolf, he maintained a close-knit circle of like-minded thinkers and artists, centered on Gordon Square where Virginia lived.

The inner circle included artists Duncan Grant and Vanessa Bell; critics Lytton Strachey, Roger Fry, and Clive Bell; as well as the economist John Maynard Keynes, though many others dropped in to share in the avant-garde buzz surrounding the group, given the added attraction of their effortlessly superior social standing. But the elitist ambience of the group, their progressive politics, and their disregard for convention— especially in personal and sexual relationships—left room for much criticism, leading to the famous comment that the group did little more than "live in squares and love in triangles."

The outcome of so much intensity and striving for a new social order was not always happiness. Virginia Woolf, after many years of mental instability, and against the background of her long-lasting love affair with the blue-blooded Vita Sackville-West, committed suicide in 1941.

Chelsea (proper noun)

An affluent area in London that is home to the annual Chelsea Flower Show.

The annual Chelsea Flower Show is reputed to be the greatest flower show on earth. It is a major event for all those men and women who have spent the entire year **pottering** (and probably potting, too) and who come out by the thousands to see how the professional garden designers fare in competition against each other. Why the general public subjects itself to this experience of acute envy is not exactly clear.

Most amateur gardeners spend a great deal of time battling against the unexpected and the unwilling—weather, plants, neighbors, and spouses. But if there is one consolation found in coming to Chelsea, it seems that the professionals have precisely the same problems: Plants fail to thrive, water features dry up or overflow, neighbors complain, workmen don't turn up on time, and trellises collapse in the wind. And still, in the end, the results can be marvelous.

Yet a word of cautionary wisdom. The writer Rudyard Kipling produced what may be the best practical comment on gardening in literature in a brief verse that goes:

Our England is a garden,
and such gardens are not made
by sighing, "Oh, how beautiful!"
and sitting in the shade.

(The) Continent (noun)

An affectionate, if slightly patronizing, expression to describe where non-Brits in Europe live.

The British are very conscious of being an island nation. On the Continent, that is, the other side of the English Channel, is where everyone else in Europe lives. There was, reportedly, a famous London newspaper headline which read, "Fog in Channel. Continent cut off."

In earlier centuries, it was considered an essential element of a young person's proper education to do the *Grand Tour* of European cities, learning something of our neighbors' artistic and cultural achievements in the process. Many British travelers fell in love with these places. Some never came back. But for most, the experience was somewhat mixed and dangerously unhealthy. The strange food, the doubtful purity of the water, the casual approach to life's little intimacies, were far too unfamiliar and uncomfortable, even life-threatening, for those of a delicate temperament. For such unsteady souls, the White Cliffs of Dover were a truly beloved sight on the return home.

For these reasons, it could be said that the moment you first stepped off a plane or boat and onto the Continent used to be a turning point in a British person's life.

Coventry, send someone to (expression)

To ostracize, ignore, shun, or treat as a pariah.

Coventry is a businesslike town in the Midlands (the area that separates the north of England from the south) that appears to have never done anyone any harm, yet the saying implies otherwise. Like so many sayings that enter popular language, this one has an uncertain origin. It may have its roots in the seventeenth century when, during the English Civil War between Royalists and Parliamentarians, any soldiers of King Charles I that were captured in the battles around the Midlands were literally sent to Coventry, a town that was loyal to Parliament. The people of Coventry were not very welcoming to these enemies and tended to ignore the disgraced soldiers, refusing to serve them in taverns or inns so they were largely reduced to begging in the streets. To be sent to Coventry, then, may have served as a threat hanging over Royalist soldiers so that they fought all the harder to avoid capture.

Unfortunately, the threat didn't have the required effect. The Parliamentarians subsequently defeated and deposed the forces of King Charles I and, in 1649, in an act that sent shockwaves around the royal courts of Europe, cut off his head. Many thought we had reached, in today's phrase, *the end of monarchy*, but it was not to be.

Dickensian (adjective)

Gloomy, squalid.

The Victorian novelist Charles Dickens (1812–70) wrote compelling works filled with vivid details of the difficult social conditions in the London of his day. The accounts in his novels of the appalling fate of the poor and the squalid conditions in prisons and poorhouses attracted much attention and increased public awareness of the terrible suffering endured by the lowest classes of society. The term *Dickensian* is still used to describe acute conditions of poverty or deprivation wherever they may be found in Britain.

DIY (noun phrase)

An abbreviation of the phrase Do-It-Yourself, referring to the maintenance, building, and repairs of the home by the homeowner, often left unfinished.

Elsewhere we examine the British national hobby of **pottering**, an activity that requires absolutely no skill at all and appeals to England's love of all that is amateur. To talk of being good at pottering, or bad at it, would be nonsense. However, bolder Englishmen who retain memories of their hunting and gathering days and feel the need to flex their muscles are drawn toward DIY, or Do-It-Yourself, endeavors.

They are drawn for economic reasons, too, as a good plumber—who earns more annually than the prime minister—will charge you a princely sum to come out and unclog your sink, a job that will take him about two minutes.

So the argument for DIY is clear: Why pay someone to do something that you can do yourself? But beware, because once you fall into the trap of thinking you can do anything with tools, you are lost. First, you will probably end up spending more on the tools and equipment than you ever did on the plumber. Second, you are likely to become one of the two hundred thousand victims of DIY accidents recorded each year in Britain. In addition, all the evidence suggests that more than one-third of DIY projects are left unfinished and professionals have to come in and fix the mess anyway.

But the tradition goes back a long way. Jerome K. Jerome, in his 1889 comic novel *Three Men in a Boat*, describes the activities of his Uncle Podger in putting up a picture, and the fear he strikes into those around him while doing so.

> *"Aunt Maria would mildly observe that next time Uncle Podger was going to hammer a nail into the wall, she hoped he'd let her know in time, so that she could make arrangements to go and spend a week with her mother."*

Yet Uncle Podger's enthusiasm never dims. As he steps back from his work around midnight and beholds the damage extending for yards around his crooked and insecure picture, he declares, "There you are. Some people would have had a man in to do a little thing like that."

There is, of course, a painless alternative for filling your leisure time. Women, much more clever than men at most things, and usually less eager to prove their handiness, identified it a long time ago. It's safe, clean, not life-threatening at all, and all you need is a credit card. It's called retail therapy.

Dog's life (expression)

In the modern context, a life of comfort and ease—like the life of the beloved family dog who snoozes by the fire and symbolizes hearth and home.

Everyone knows that we Brits treat our dogs better than our children, and we are often reminded that the Society for the Prevention of Cruelty to Animals was founded in 1824, sixty years before the National Society for the Prevention of Cruelty to Children. Is it deeply meaningful that the SPCA went on to become the Royal Society (RSPCA) while the children's society still waits for that honor?

What, then, lies behind this remarkable but apparently sincere attachment we have to our dogs? The truth is, we seem more able to freely express ourselves with animals than we are with other people. Kate Fox, the British social commentator, pondering on this aspect of the Brits' relationship with their pets, explains convincingly, "unlike our fellow Englishmen, animals are not embarrassed or put off by our **un-English** displays of emotion."

The word *dog* itself is peculiarly native to Britain and comes from an obscure Old English past. The alternative Germanic term, *hound*, refers mainly to hunting dogs. In feudal society, such dogs might be given special treatment by their lordly master and be fed from his table. But lesser dogs out in the yard had a rougher time, and our language is crammed with phrases suggesting that a dog's life, at least up to the nineteenth century, was a miserable fate: *dog-tired*, *dogsbody*, *going to the dogs*, *die like a dog*, and so on. For the most part, dogs were treated with contempt and sometimes cruelty. Even the question, "What was it like?" might produce the answer, "An absolute dog!" No positive qualities here, then.

In curious contrast, the modern reality is that the British treat dogs with huge affection, looking on them as beloved companions and having lifelong bonds with them. The British adore the legendary image of a dog's faithfulness and literal doggedness.

Nature seems to provide plenty of evidence to justify this attitude. Endless anecdotes suggest that dogs are strangely and deeply attuned to their owners, with some observers believing their pets have psychic powers. The researcher and scientist Rupert Sheldrake, for example, has conducted surveys to demonstrate that dogs (among other pets) waiting at home *know* the moment their owners leave the office and begin their homeward journey.

So what is a British dog's life like these days? Some commentators think the sense of the phrase has gradually changed and now means to have a cosseted and comfortable existence, rather than the opposite. I am quite sure the Queen's corgis would agree with that.

However, this cozy impression is not borne out by our behavior in the real world. According to a 2013 survey, the incidence of stray and abandoned dogs in England was estimated at around 111,000. What's going on here? Two extremes of behavior meeting in a confused national psyche? It does seem that, in their attitudes to animals and children, we find one of the paradoxes of the British temperament.

All the same, there is one common expression which continues to suggest a bond between human and animal that is more than mere friendship: "Love me, love my dog." Or rather, in practice, "Love my dog, love me." Watch dog owners meeting in a public park and you will see how it works. Better than a dating agency any time.

First cuckoo (noun phrase)

The sound of the first cuckoo means that spring has arrived and that Brits have begun to dream, in vain, of warm weather.

There is a persistent myth that an annual event occurs in the Letters to the Editor column of *The Times* (London), when someone writes to announce the date when they heard "the first cuckoo," as these birds migrate to Britain for the summer.

The Times has gone to some trouble, however, to publicize the fact that they do not print readers' letters on this subject.

"According to our digital archive we haven't actually published a straightforward 'first cuckoo' letter since 1940," declares their correspondent, Sally Baker. Even more assertively, she adds, "I, too, extend a warm welcome, wherever he or she presently is, to the first cuckoo of this spring. But please, don't tell us about it."

Even when this tradition was at its height, it seems that doubts entered the journalistic mind. The following Letter to the Editor, from a Mr. Fydekker, is dated February 12, 1913:

> Sir, I regret to say that, in common with many other persons, I have been completely deceived in the matter of the supposed cuckoo of February 4. The note was uttered by a bricklayer's laborer at work on a house. I have interviewed the man, who tells me that he is able to draw cuckoos from considerable distances by the exactness of his imitation of their notes.

It has been suggested that these *first cuckoo* records are a useful indicator of climate change but the increasingly early emergence of the bumblebee from hibernation—previously never before February, but now active as early as December— appears to be a far more dramatic sign of global warming.

Gazump (verb)

An unethical practice by home sellers whereby the price of a piece of real estate is raised after the sale has been agreed upon but before the contract is signed.

Usually so proud of their reputation for playing fair, the English have a curious blind spot when it comes to buying and selling houses. A seller gazumps on the pretext that he or she has received a higher offer elsewhere. The original buyer is then forced to raise his or her offer or the property goes to the higher bidder. This unethical, but not illegal, practice appeared first with the spelling *gazoomph* and was derived from an older and more general term *gazumph* (or *gezumph*) for the various kinds of swindling that occur at dishonest auctions.

Gone for a Burton (expression)

Expression from the Second World War to describe an airman who was killed or had gone missing.

Beer and the military have a long and happy association that goes back many centuries. A common euphemism used in the Second World War, especially with RAF pilots, was the phrase *Gone for a Burton*, used to describe fellow airmen who were killed or had gone missing. Burton, here, refers to a well-known beer that originated in the Midlands town of Burton-on-Trent. Though no one can quite pin down the origin of this phrase, I like the theory that it came from a series of beer advertisements in the interwar years, each showing a picture of a sports team with a gap where one member is missing, and the tag line underneath reads "Gone for a Burton." The Burton Brewery itself was no longer operating under that name in the 1940s, but the Burton style of strong, dark beer was still widely enjoyed, and would certainly have been known in air force messes and bars around the country.

Gone west is another phrase associated with war. Put briefly, *to go west* is "to die." We find it in use by both soldiers and airmen during the First World War, to describe being sent back from the trenches, thus sent westward, usually with fatal injuries, as minor wounds were treated in the battle area. But the concept has much older associations in ancient spirituality. Because the sun went down over the western ocean, there was the tradition, both in Christian and pagan European thought, that the soul's journey to its ultimate end lay "westwards."

Ha-ha (noun)

Eccentric British word for laughter. Also, a kind of wall.

This odd noun, meaning a kind of wall, is quintessentially British and tells us a lot about ourselves. **Ha-ha** is the British onomatopoeic word for laughter, and the name is supposed to arise from the humorous reaction of people when they first see a ha-ha wall. But what's funny about a wall?

It all has to do with the British and our love–hate relationship with nature. As with our attitude to animals and children, our response to nature is rather confused: We spend an equal amount of time walking through it as we do building over it. To the modern suburban gardener, nature is the enemy (see **pottering**), but historically, this has not always been the case. If we go back to the seventeenth and eighteenth centuries, we find the earliest signs of what was to become the Romantic movement, reasserting humankind's closeness to nature as a source of beauty, feeling, and inspiration. Usually this is taken to be a reaction to the cerebral rationalism of the Enlightenment. But the British were never quite so persuaded as the French, for instance, that reason was the beginning and end of everything. As with most important matters, the British retained an amateur approach, especially in the activity of thinking. This allowed them to dabble and remain slightly out of control in philosophical issues. And in their gardens, too. While the French created Versailles, with its clipped hedges and symmetrical patterns, the British created undulating parks that took nature as it was and just reorganized it slightly. Marie Antoinette so liked this idea (she had problems adapting to stuffy old Versailles, anyway) that she created her own *jardin anglais*, a secret place where all the French rules were broken, and plants and trees were allowed, within limits, to be themselves.

Back to the ha-ha. So devoted were us British to our rolling hills and natural estates, that we decided we would like to sit in our homes and see it all unfurl before us. But traditional walls got in the way, obstructing our views of the beauty beyond. Hence, someone had the bright idea of bordering the home-garden with a sunken wall, keeping out the livestock and the deer, while allowing an open and uninterrupted view. An invisible wall. No wonder people exclaimed "ha-ha!" when they first saw it.

Jumble sale (noun)

A traditional sale involving a mixture of items donated by members of a church or community as a way of fund-raising.

Jumble is a curious little word that has done a lot of traveling in its time, starting out as a verb meaning something like *stumble* or *tumble*, then denoting sexual activity, as tumble still does. However, it reinvented itself as a noun in the seventeenth century, meaning a "confused mixture." It is defined that way in the 1755 volume of Samuel Johnson's *Dictionary of the English Language*, with the added sense of "violent or confused agitation." All this brings us to the wonderful tradition of the jumble sale, a delightfully confused mixture of items all donated by members of a church or community as a way of fundraising. The jumble sale is where the British spirit of optimism reigns supreme, always hoping to turn up some precious antique among the pile of discarded items brought out from the attic after years of neglect.

Manor (noun)

A large, elegant residence, or the principal house on an estate in rural Britain, ruled over by the lord of the manor.

The English language has a huge debt to French, in particular to our Norman conquerors of the eleventh century, who in one fell swoop brought us veal, pork, beef, mutton, venison, castles, domains, and last but not least, manors. The references to meat, by the way, come from the fact that these are the

French-derived terms for the food served at the table to our foreign overlords. Meanwhile, the English-speaking serfs and peasants continued to raise pigs, cows, goats, and sheep.

Manor comes directly from the French *manoir,* in its turn from the Latin *manere,* "to stay." The feudal pattern, working like a pyramid from the poorest at the bottom, through various degrees of privilege all the way to the ruler at the top, was based entirely on land ownership and the income it provided. At a local level, the tenure of land was granted to the "lord of the manor," or *seigneur,* whose tenants actually worked the fields. This simple arrangement, enshrined in the *Domesday Book*—the written record of the great census ordered by William the Conqueror in 1086—was to establish the character of rural Britain for centuries to follow. Even now, families exist that have manorial rights going back hundreds of years, and manors continue to be bought and sold, along with their titles.

Borrowing from this strong sense of ownership, the Londoner talks of his or her manor, namely, their corner or village in the metropolis—even if it lacks the grandeur of the original meaning.

Middle England (noun phrase)

A term that refers to the socio-economic middle and lower-middle classes of England that are typically more right-wing.

A phrase often on the lips of politicians and pollsters, by which they mean the middle bit of England that is at the center of the voting spectrum. Middle England, it has been said, has its spiritual home in Tunbridge Wells, a town in Kent which is carefully conservative in its outlook.

"What comes to mind when you think of Tunbridge Wells?" asked the BBC back in 1999. "Doilies, Women's Institute, semi-detached, cricket on the green, retired colonels, bone china, bridge evenings, perhaps?" In other words, all the trappings of a more genteel past, redolent with Georgian and Victorian elegance and well-being. "It stands for everything that made Britain great, before the ghastly dawn of unemployment, drug abuse, foul-mouthed disrespectful youth, and teenage single mothers." There are many who would agree with that, though there certainly is a tone of idealism in this statement as well. (See **manners makyth man**)

Old **Blighty** (noun phrase)

An affectionate term for Britain, commonly used at the beginning of the First World War and featured in popular marching songs.

Old Blighty, sometimes just *Blighty*, derives from military slang dating from the Indian campaigns of the nineteenth century. *Blighty* was the British soldier's corruption of the Hindi word *bilayati*, meaning "foreign." In their Anglo-Indian dictionary of 1886, Yule and Burnell say that the word referred to a number of unfamiliar products that the British brought with them.

The expression came into common use as a term for Britain at the beginning of the First World War. It is nearly always associated with the soldier's sense of loss and nostalgia for the old country and turns up in popular marching songs. It appears, too, in the lines of war poets such as Siegfried Sassoon and Wilfred Owen, most poignantly in the latter's poem "The Dead-Beat" where a soldier in the trenches goes into a state of shock and refuses to move, staring into nothingness. A low voice says, "It's Blighty, p'raps, he sees."

Oxbridge (proper noun)

Shorthand or slang for the universities of Oxford and Cambridge.

Familiarly known as Oxbridge, Oxford and Cambridge need no introduction as world famous centers of tradition and excellence. These bastions of privilege are always in competition with one another and always on top of the game in the attraction they hold for students going on to university.

Where would we be without Oxbridge, either to love or condemn for its undisputed image of privilege and prestige? For many, its picture of gilded youth is still the blissful, dreamy setting depicted in Evelyn Waugh's *Brideshead Revisited*; an endless summer of college gardens, boating, riverside pubs, and genial servants clearing up the mess after one's excesses. But those days are long gone and the fictional descriptions always forgot to mention the ferociously cold winter climate of both cities, much less the harsh reality of living in medieval buildings without any plumbing. The plumbing, however, is much improved, and along with other modernizing influences, the exquisitely photogenic background has these days become more the down-to-earth style of Inspector Morse than the quail's egg breakfasts of Sebastian Flyte.

In the real world, Oxbridge still represents a place of forging connections and friendships for life, and with competition for jobs ever more fierce, it may ease the path to a career after graduating, if a career is really what you want after such an exalted education. (See **old school tie**)

Pottering (noun, verb)

The art of patrolling and improving one's garden in one's spare time.

Visitors to Britain are often amazed by the thousands of houses lining little streets, many of them dating back to Georgian or Victorian times. "Where are the tower blocks?" they want to know. There are, of course, residential tower blocks, many of them dating from the 1960s and 1970s. These days, of course, we realize that building them was a terrible mistake and are knocking them all down. Why is that? Because they are not really British. You can't potter in a tower block, and pottering is our most important national pastime, usually taking up several hours a week, and after retirement even several hours daily.

Do not be misled into thinking that pottering means filling your time in trifling ways—it is a national occupation. We go to work to earn money so we can come home and potter. However (and this is why you have to earn the money), you need a garden to potter in. A piece of British earth that is your own. This is every British person's dream.

So when you hear that lovely expression "An Englishman's home is his castle," it actually means "An Englishman's garden is his castle." No feature of British life gives more happiness and sense of security, or more tension with one's neighbors than a garden. This green oasis is an expression of your own personality, to be defended at all costs from every type of threat. These include Mr. Smith's cat, Mrs. Johnson's terrier that gets through the fence, and, above all, Mr. Smith and Mrs. Johnson themselves, who may get the idea in their heads to build an extension, put up a high fence or wall, cut down a tree, set up a barbecue right next to your hedge and so invade your space with the smell of burned steak or, heaven forbid, plant fast-growing conifers that will steal your sunlight!

Quite clearly, though, the primeval enemy of the suburban garden is nature itself (but see **ha-ha** for other attitudes), and this is where pottering becomes a vital pursuit. As we say, the price of freedom is eternal vigilance. Nature must be watched at all times. So pottering is a kind of routine security procedure, demanding the closest attention to very small things like ants and beetles, as well as to the activities of larger enemies, such as rabbits, moles, squirrels, and pigeons. No stone must be left unturned in the search for slugs, no flowering border left unexamined in case an alien creature has penetrated the sanctuary. A lifetime can be spent improving the boundary defenses and constructing paths that enable you to rush to the site of an emergency. All of this is very costly in terms of time and money, but absolutely essential for our national security.

Raining cats and dogs (expression)

Raining harder than usual and definitely necessitating the wearing of **wellies***. A common occurrence in England.*

No book on England would be complete without mentioning the weather, and our green and pleasant land owes much of its greenness and pleasantness to rain.

As many visitors discover, a British summer is no guarantee of sun, hence our obsession with the Mediterranean as a holiday destination, and why we tend to leave just as you are arriving. Nothing personal. At any time though, a downpour can wash out a picnic or a sporting event, no matter how important, and whether Wimbledon or Lord's, the rain shows a total disrespect for international tennis and cricket. I imagine that Shakespeare's open-air Globe theater frequently suffered the same fate, perhaps inspiring Feste's lament at the end of *Twelfth Night* that "the rain it raineth every day"?

We spend a lot of time wondering about rain (will it? won't it?), and complaining about it when it does. Rain for the English is thus the same as snow for the Inuit and commands a wide range of vocabulary including: *drizzle, shower, spit, pour, deluge, pelt, torrent, cloudburst, downpour,* as well as the more graphic metaphors, *to rain buckets, pitchforks,* and then *cats and dogs.*

The *buckets* are plain enough, and *pitchforks* one can more or less imagine, but *cats and dogs?* We find an early seventeenth-century reference to "raining dogs and polecats," and some ninety years later Jonathan Swift gives us, "he was sure it would rain cats and dogs."

But the true origin of the expression is obscure. Could it really come from Norse sea lore associating the spirits of cats with rain and dogs with wind? Unlikely. Or is it rhyming slang for *raining frogs?* (Which can happen, but only once in a blue moon.) Or, when it poured down in earlier times, did city dwellers literally see the streets awash with dead cats and dogs, as Swift's poem "Description of a City Shower" tells us? There seems no better theory to offer than poor drainage and a plague of unfortunate stray animals.

Semi-detached (noun, adjective)

A modest and ubiquitous home type in Britain built adjoining the next-door neighbor on one side for reasons of economy and space.

An Englishman's home may be his castle, as the saying goes, but in practice a great number of British homes are semi-detached, that is, they are built adjoining the next-door neighbor on one side. The revealing thing about this word is that we never say semi-attached even though it is probably nearer the truth.

By extension, one of the worst things you can say about anyone is that, "he leads a semi-detached life in the suburbs of London."

Ploughman's Lunch

British food and drink may not be the most sophisticated in the world, but it's comforting and familiar (and even better when washed down with a **pint of bitter** or a **nice cup of tea**). Brits pride themselves on not making a fuss, and the food and drink they love most is simple, hearty fare. Think cheese sandwiches or fish and **chips** and you won't go wrong. The idea is that fancy restaurants are all well and good, but it's less risky and just as enjoyable to cook in the comfort of your own home, or pop down to the **local pub** for a meal. Cheers!

Bangers 'n' mash (noun)

A substantial meal of sausages and mashed potatoes, often served with onion gravy. Great for soaking up beer and a staple on British pub menus.

Fortunate children all over the world grow up with comforting memories of certain meals; good, solid food served at the family table that symbolizes nourishment and security. For British children, bangers 'n' mash is one of those memorable meals, like fish 'n' chips, but much more associated with home cooking than with take-out food.

Bangers is a slang term for sausages that goes back at least one hundred years, but is of uncertain origin. *Mash* is mashed potatoes, though more widely the word *mash* can be used to mean any vegetable or grain mashed up with hot water, originally as feed for animals.

Every family once had its favorite recipe for this dish, either in the ingredients for the rich onion gravy or in the mash preparation.

Binge-drinking (noun, verb)

The consumption of large amounts of alcohol in a short time, which, in England, usually leads to rude and antisocial behavior such as swearing and brawling.

The reputation of the British *lager lout*—an aggressively drunk young male—has spread across Europe. Their bad behavior was at its height in the 1990s when a British vice consul in Ibiza, Spain, resigned his post in disgust over their nightly antics. But what are we to make of the *Rough Guide to England* verdict from May 2008 that the English as a whole are a nation of "overweight, binge-drinking, reality TV addicts, obsessed with **toffs** and C-list celebs"? That's rather severe, surely? Not all of us are overweight.

Bottoms up (expression)

A colloquial variation on the word cheers. Typically used when drinking socially.

When it was our turn to rule the world and we needed a lot of ships and men to police it, there was a constant call for recruitment to the navy. Life at sea was not attractive for a simple seaman (or *jack tar*), and there were no union representatives or lawyers on board to say, "Please stop flogging that man." So persuading healthy young men to join up was not an easy task. As a result, the navy resorted to trickery. So-called *press gangs* went around to dockside pubs and bought drinks for the unwary. The trick was that at the bottom of the pewter pot was a coin, and on finishing the drink you automatically "took the King's shilling," thus you agreed to join up.

As people became aware of this trap, pubs began to sell alcohol in glass bottom pewter pots to make the coin visible. As you lifted the tankard, you could then see the coin against the glass bottom. Hence the expression *bottoms up*, which continues to be used as a happy exhortation to drink up.

Chips (noun)

French fries, Brit-style! Thicker and heavier than the American version, they are eaten with almost anything from bacon and eggs to an Indian curry.

It is an ironic development that, while some social researchers are discovering that we can be "surprisingly patriotic and enthusiastic about the humble chip," (which, incidentally, originated in Belgium), other reports declare that our national dish is no longer fish and chips, but instead, the Great British Curry—specifically a variation on chicken tikka masala, which originated in the Indian subcontinent.

There can be no doubt, though, that our relationship with fish and chips is deeply and permanently established, at least as long as there are fish in the sea. Long before McDonald's appeared on the British scene, we had a take-out fish and chip shop in almost every town and village in the country.

The humble chip has even entered literature, as in Arnold Wesker's semiautobiographical 1962 play, *Chips with Everything*. This is Wesker's story of a national service conscript, the son of a general, trying to fit in with his fellow conscripts of working class background. The young soldier finds himself at odds not only with them, but also with the officer class that his own background should make his natural allies. The dumbing down formula of *Chips with Everything* reflects the tortured class relations so typical of English institutions, and the impossible struggle of the main character to redefine his identity in his own right.

Elevens (noun)

A drink and small snack consumed around eleven o'clock in the morning to bridge the gap between breakfast and lunch.

The simple identification of a time of day with a snack seems logical enough. In the English world, elevenses are eaten at eleven o'clock in the morning, and usually consist of a cup of tea or coffee and some sweet accompaniment in the form of cake or cookies. One thing is clear—without the solid food, the occasion would only be tea or coffee and not elevenses.

And here it all starts to get mysterious. I can't find any explanation for why there are elevenses but no oneses, fourses,

or sixes. There may be a connection with the eating habits
of the British in the Indian Raj, when elevenses presented an
opportunity for an early aperitif (plus, of course, the obligatory
cake or cookies), with *tiffin,* or "light lunch," following from one
o'clock onward.

Local pub (noun)

*A vital British institution, traditionally visited at least once a week for
a drink and a good chat. Usually cozy and welcoming, like a favorite
pair of old socks.*

At the very center of British village life, the local pub is
traditionally not only a social club, but also a haven for
the lonely and weary, a welcome for the traveler, and an
intelligence hub for all that is going on in the village. As
our major cities sprang up, the tradition of the local pub
transferred to urban life as well. The large conurbation often
swallowed up older towns and villages, which, to some extent,
kept their local character.

The *lounge bar*, the *public bar,* and the *snug* are the names
of different areas of a traditional pub, dating from earlier
times. When workmen on their way home from their trades
and labors wanted to pop in for a pint in their working clothes,
they went to the *public bar*, a "spit-and-sawdust" area where
the furniture was bare wood and the floor uncarpeted. Those
wanting a more genteel evening out went to the *lounge bar*,
where they paid a little extra for their drinks in order to
have cushioned seats or benches, carpet on the floor, and a
supposedly higher standard of decor. The *snug* was a tiny space,

often between the two bars, where a couple could squeeze in and have a little privacy.

Traditionally, drinking hours were strictly controlled. Around 11 P.M. the landlord rings a bell and gives his customers ten minutes drinking-up time to down their drinks and leave the premises in an orderly fashion. In more remote places there survives the discreet tradition of the *lock-in*, where a select group of the landlord's regulars are allowed to stay on and drink after the doors are shut and the curtains drawn. The relaxation of licensing hours was supposed to have ended this practice, but it is so delightfully illicit that I am sure it continues.

However, these days pubs seem to be in trouble. The British Beer and Pub Association claims pub beer sales are at half the level they were in 1979. And—according to CAMRA (the Campaign for Real Ale)—pubs are closing at the rate of sixty per month. Country pubs seem the hardest hit, with the recent ban on smoking and severe penalties for drunk-driving making people more inclined to drink at home. For many pubs, survival depends on encouraging families to eat out. The Mitchell and Butler pub chain says that food sales account for thirty-seven percent of their turnover, compared with beer at thirty-one percent. The onus seems to be on publicans, then, to work at improving their food and at losing the terrible label that overpriced and poor quality *pub grub* has acquired over the years.

Alternatively, with so many small village shops and post offices closing around the country, the suggestion has come from no less than Prince Charles, heir to the throne, that country pubs, in a new initiative for survival, could combine all these roles in one. Such a change could alter the perception of the "local" in a big way.

Meat and potatoes (expression)

Straightforward, with no artifice, just like traditional British fare (see **bangers 'n' mash***).*

A heartwarming and enjoyable expression, full of nourishment, and with a sturdy reality to it. To be a *meat and potatoes* man is to be one who is unconcerned with frills and fancies, a straightforward kind of guy. Meanwhile the *meat and potatoes* of a book, or a text, or an agreement, is the basic and most fundamental part. The phrase appears to date from the middle of the twentieth century and may convey something of the post-war shortages in Britain, at a time when meat was still rationed and a proper meal was considered to be made up of both protein and carbohydrates. Other rugby-team-style meanings have been suggested to me for this expression, which I cannot possibly begin to explore, this being a decent family book.

Nice cup of tea (expression)

The preparation and consumption of tea in the correct manner. One of the mainstays of British civilization.

Reports say that Britons drink anything between one hundred thirty and one hundred sixty million cups of tea each day, though who has been out there counting them, I have no idea. It is comforting, though, for all those tea lovers so long considered unsexy, to read *Thelondonpaper's* November 2006 report that "Tea is the new coffee. It seems that with the approval of stellar names such as Kate Moss, Daniel Craig, and

Stella McCartney, teahouses are fast becoming the place to be seen in the capital."

So the great wheel of history turns. For the celebrity tea habit goes back to seventeenth-century Britain when, in imitation of the racy, liberal tea-drinking monarch Charles II, teahouses sprang up in London and became the fashionable venue for sophisticated people to gather.

As for a nice cup of tea, well, that is another matter. The Japanese do it their way, with ritual and ceremony, but the British are no less fussy. There is *tea*, and there is a *nice cup of tea*. To show how seriously this matter is taken, George Orwell published a 1946 article in the *Evening Standard*, entitled, "A Nice Cup of Tea," where he asserts that "tea is one of the mainstays of civilization in this country." When he looks through his own recipe for tea, he says, "I find no fewer than eleven outstanding points," and goes on to enumerate his rules, "every one of which I regard as golden."

In its generic form, tea is quite classless, yet if we compare the practice of tea making in the average truck (or lorry) drivers' cafe with the beverage served by Lady Muck-Worthington to the local vicar, there is a world of difference. So what for the truck driver is *a decent cuppa* (as they say, a spoon will stand up in it), will certainly not appeal to the president of the Women's Institute.

"Just my/your cup of tea" expresses without ambiguity what your flavor is, whether in things, places, or people. "Surrey is a very different cup of tea from Kent" reinforces a contrast. And in the form "Not my cup of tea," we hear a very British type of judgment, not too severe, not too condemnatory, but firm and telling all the same.

Pint of bitter (noun)

A pint of English ale, served lukewarm and proudly imbibed by Brits who consider it to be the best alcoholic beverage in the entire world.

As the rest of Europe knows all too well, England (in the form of the UK Government) has fought hard to keep certain traditions untouched by the bureaucratic hand of Brussels. Well, if the French can do it for cheese and farmers, why can't the British do it for beer, our national drink? And so the pint of bitter, with its popular blend of hops and malt, continues to be served in English pubs in defiance of metric measurement standards.

In September 2007, after years of wrangling and complaining, the European Commission finally gave up the struggle. Günter Verheugen, the EU Industry Commissioner, declared, "I want to bring to an end a bitter, bitter battle that has lasted for decades and which in my view is completely pointless." He seems to have been completely unaware of the dreadful pun on *bitter* in his statement.

Yet beer-drinking habits have undergone much change in recent years, according to a survey from brewery giant SABMiller. This is mainly due to long working hours for the British, as many work up to forty-eight hours per week. Regular lunchtime drinking is a thing of the past, with only one in ten Britons enjoying a midday pint. And we start drinking later in the evening than any of our European neighbors. At 6:14 P.M. to be precise, the report says.

Ploughman's lunch (noun)

A simple pub meal of bread and cheese.

This phrase from pub menus has an attractive ring to it, intentionally. In reality meaning nothing more than bread and cheese, garnished with a bit of salad, it conjures up the hearty fare of country inns and images of the rugged countryman and his earthy lifestyle. But we find a darker layer to the phrase in the 1983 movie, *The Ploughman's Lunch*, based on a story written by Ian McEwan. During a pub meal with a friend, the term *ploughman's lunch* is exposed as a mere marketing gimmick to sell a simple product at an inflated price. The movie is an ironic and bleak comment on how modern commercial practices threaten an older pattern of British life, taking over and exploiting terms like *traditional, country,* and *home* in their advertising and labeling.

Shandy (noun)

A popular drink of beer mixed with lemonade or ginger beer.

Shandy is a common abbreviation for *shandygaff*, a beer mixed with lemonade or ginger beer, first recorded in the nineteenth century, and of unknown origin. As a light drink, a shandy is popular with sports players because it allows you to refresh yourself after exertion and drink alcohol at the same time. Note that the traditional British mix uses ginger beer, not ginger ale.

Secondly, and more importantly in the history of English words, Tristram Shandy is the eponymous hero and narrator of Laurence Sterne's riotous and confusing eighteenth-century novel that was written as a broadside against rationalism.

Never has a book leaned so much on nonsense, non sequiturs, and spontaneous distractions from the plot. Sterne adored playing with language and he was a compulsive lover and inventor of words with a number of first attributions in *The Oxford English Dictionary* to his name, including *lackadaisical, whimsicality, muddle-headed, good-tempered*, and *sixth sense*. Writing for many years from the timeless tranquillity of Yorkshire villages, he later spent some of his final years traveling in Europe for the sake of his health, recording his impressions in a second novel, *A Sentimental Journey Through France and Italy*. When he died in 1768, Sterne left behind a legacy of wordplay and sheer zest for invention and innuendo, which has given us an entire genre of extempore writing, exemplified by authors like James Joyce.

Nowt So Queer As Folk

Britain is known for its venerable history and picturesque scenery but for many, it's the eccentric inhabitants that make it truly "great." Take a stroll through any British town and you'll find a host of colorful characters. You may meet an **anorak**, an **egghead**, a **toff**, or even a **twitcher**, far from its native habitat. If you're a fan of Britain and its "queer folk," read on and enjoy!

Anorak (noun)

A sloppy, unattractive waterproof coat and a slang word for a person who is gray and colorless, such as a politician.

In its original sense, an anorak is an item of weatherproof clothing, usually with a hood and drawstrings, apparently copied from a kind of Inuit clothing worn in the Arctic. But in its widely used slang meaning, an *anorak* is a person obsessively engaged in a detailed activity of absolutely no interest to *normal* people. The association probably came about through the fact that trainspotters, people who stand for hours at railway stations collecting the engine numbers of locomotives as they pass, tended to wear warm, outdoor clothing such as anoraks.

The slack, sloppy appearance of the anorak garment, as far removed from elegance and sophistication as can be imagined, came to represent the supposedly rather dull and unimaginative personality of the wearer. No doubt this is an unfair generalization, but anyone who has found himself trapped on a railway car with an anorak—the person, not the garment—as I was on the occasion of the final journey of an old steam locomotive, might well reach such a conclusion.

Anoraks appear in public life, too. In the 1990s British Prime Minister John Major was considered by the media to be a gray and colorless individual. A popular political cartoon of the day by Patrick Wright shows *101 Uses for a John Major*, with one "use" depicting him as a trainspotter's anorak. (See also **naff**)

Bluestocking (noun)

A patronizing word once used by British gentlemen to describe women who had aspirations of intellectual equality with men.

Since the eighteenth century both British society and literature have been strongly influenced by the struggle of women to be recognized for their intelligence as well as their beauty and needlework skills. So it must be all the more discouraging for women that the label *bluestocking*, at present referring mostly to female academics or intellectuals, should still carry a negative connotation.

The term came into use in London in the 1750s with the creation of a literary discussion group by high society ladies wanting to follow the example of French *salons*, (often hosted by influential aristocratic women) as well as the French women's group known as *Bas bleu*. The British group may well have referred to themselves informally as the Blue Stocking Society, but an early use of the name seems to have come dismissively from one of the ladies' husbands who was not at all impressed with his wife's cultured friends and their literary pretensions.

Why the French should have been able to establish such a strong *salon* tradition led by women, while British female society was left struggling for intellectual equality with men, reflects a certain difference between the two cultures of the time. British women went on to plead their case mainly through the medium of the novel. As the famous and pithy quote from Jane Austen's *Northanger Abbey* goes, "A woman especially, if she have the misfortune of knowing anything, should conceal it as well as she can."

Bobby (noun)

An old-fashioned term for the kindly British police officer of yesteryear.

Any visitor to Britain should know the best form of address for a police officer. After all, you never know when you might want help. But care is needed here. You might think you were being polite if you walked up and said, "Excuse me, officer," but most police, unused to such respectful treatment, would think you were "taking the mickey."

Conversation about the police these days is confused by there being so many slang words for them, ranging from the rather outdated *bobby* or *copper*, to more recent terms like *the fuzz*, *the filth*, and *the Bill*. Let's start from the beginning.

Bobby is an old-fashioned term for the British police dating from the early nineteenth century when Sir Robert (Bob) Peel introduced the first police force to London. (In the capital they were also once known as *peelers*.) Traditionally, the bobby was a figure of local support and help, belonging to a past when parents always said to children, "If you're ever in trouble, ask a policeman." In more modern times, *the fuzz, the Bill*, or *the old Bill*, all in general use, also seem to be inoffensive.

Sadly, the bobby image of the police has suffered much since the 1960s when, instead of setting up a separate semi-military force for crowd control, as in many other European countries, the government obliged ordinary policemen to don armor and weapons and bash the rioting British into submission. Since then, there have arisen more unpleasant terms for the police, especially among the young.

The police have struggled hard to regain their community image. But even now, as I observed recently in a residential area of central London, they do give mixed messages. Walking in front of me was a heavily armed policeman wearing a stab-proof jacket, with aggressive equipment of every type strapped to his chest and belt, and a large label on his back reading "Community Police."

So how would I address a police officer in the street? I think in practice I would just be polite and avoid any form of address.

British bulldog (noun phrase)

A national symbol of Great Britain resembling the famous wartime leader Sir Winston Churchill and denoting strength, stubbornness, and tenacity.

The British bulldog motif will be familiar to every tourist visiting London, and it evokes, yet again, that image the British have of themselves as resilient, strong, and when provoked, with a nasty bite. The national self-image is all the more confirmed when we consider that Sir Winston Churchill, our famous wartime leader, was as close in looks to a bulldog as a human can possibly be.

British bulldog is also the name of a rather violent schoolyard game that British and Commonwealth children play, asserting the "tough" image of the British bulldog.

Cut a dash (expression)

Dressed to impress or dressed in one's finest attire with the aim of making a sartorial impression.

The sense is clear: to appear in public dressed up in a way that is striking. But English is a very strange language sometimes. Imagine trying to explain to a classroom of people learning English the meaning of either *cut* or *dash* that is used here. The meanings of these words bear no relation to showy dress, and we can only find echoes of sayings such as "the cut of his cloth." Brewer, in his *Dictionary of Phrase and Fable*, connects the phrase to the French *coup* (stroke) via "to make a masterly stroke."

Doolally (adjective)

Anglo-Indian expression meaning someone who is a little bit crazy or not quite right in the head.

It is not every day that you conquer an entire subcontinent. The British military and cultural triumphs in India were crowned with Queen Victoria being declared Empress of India in 1877. And as a direct result of this bold move, the Queen's English went on to be enriched by some seventy years of Anglo-Indian expressions inspired by colonial and military slang.

In case we think it was easy to govern a subcontinent with all its different races, languages, religions, and unfamiliar customs, there is plenty of evidence to suggest that the administrators and soldiers of the Raj were under a lot of mental pressure. One colorful expression that has survived is "to go doolally," in other words go slightly round the bend. It comes from the name Deolali, a military camp one hundred twenty-five miles northeast of Bombay, where the British Army had an asylum for weary and demoralized troops. Soldiers often spent months there before being sent home to England, and when they arrived back in **Old Blighty** it was obvious from their fragile state of mind that they had "gone to Deolali."

I have also heard from those with old India connections, that the expression "to go round the bend" came from the same source, being the orientation of the railway line from Bombay to Nashik Road, the local station for Deolali. This is as good a theory as any, and certainly beats the notion that Victorian mental hospitals had a bend in their driveways to distinguish them from private homes. Crazy, indeed.

Eavesdropper (noun)

A person who listens in on private conversations while remaining hidden, officially frowned upon by Brits but commonly practiced.

Before gutters and street drains were in common use, houses had wide eaves to allow rain to fall far from the walls and windows. Going right back to Old English, this extended roof was known first as the *eavesdrip*, and later as *eavesdrop*. A passerby, standing under the eavesdrop, would be likely to hear conversations from within the house without the knowledge of those inside. Hence eavesdroppers were those who listened in to private conversations. In the British code of behavior, this simply isn't done, except of course, these days, in the interests of national security.

Egghead (noun)

Affectionate and mildly derogatory term for someone who is academic and rather eccentric.

The British are, if anything, rather self-deprecating, at least on the surface. They also have a particular distrust of clever people (compare the loaded implication of the word *intellectual* in English with the admiring sense of *intellectuel* in French). Note, too, the British criticisms often used for a bright person, "Too clever for their own good," or "Too clever by half." We have no national system for honoring clever people in general in the same way as say, the French Academy.

A *boffin*, in contrast, is a dedicated scientist who pays the price of exceptional intelligence by being considered rather eccentric. The classic portrait of Albert Einstein with his hair all over the place is a perfect illustration of a boffin. Naturally, one with so much hair could never be considered an egghead.

English rose (noun)

A type of classic English beauty.

This is not a flower, but rather a winsome description of a kind of British feminine beauty ideal characterized by delicate skin with shades of white and pink. Heroines of romantic novels of a certain period would certainly qualify as English roses. However, with the arrival of sunny, Mediterranean beach vacations and the dedicated pursuit of tanned skin, this once sought-after complexion is on the decline. Yet for some, the dream remains.

'Er indoors (catchphrase)

'Er meaning "her," this catchphrase refers to a wife, or she who stays indoors.

TV soaps and series lend their catchphrases to the language just as radio did in its day. Those phrases that catch on and become popular tend to reveal something about the attitudes and sense of humor of the British. For example, "'Er indoors" is a phrase from the TV comedy series *Minder* where it was used by Arthur Daley—the lead character—to refer to his wife who is never seen in the show. Arthur is a wheeler-dealer who dabbles so much in shady business that he has to hire a *minder*, London slang for bodyguard.

A few other TV catchphrases have lodged in day-to-day speech in recent years:

"I've started so I'll finish." The frequent cry of Magnus Magnusson chairing the quiz program, *Mastermind*, as a bell sounded the end of the permitted time.

"Didn't he/she do well!" The phrase often used by Bruce Forsyth, emcee of *The Generation Game*.

"Don't mention the war." A warning from Basil Fawlty, a neurotic hotel owner, to his staff about the presence of German guests staying in the hotel, in the comedy series *Fawlty Towers*.

"Am I bovvered?" is the cry of Catherine Tate, playing her very modern teenage character Lauren who isn't *bothered*, that is, doesn't really care about much at all.

Goody Two Shoes (noun phrase)

A derogatory nickname for a female who is a little too pious and loves to do good, but in an annoying way.

There is a down-to-earth streak in the British character that, while it recognizes good qualities, is quickly turned off by smugness and pompous virtue. In an anonymously authored eighteenth-century morality tale for children, *The History of Little Goody Two Shoes*, Goody Two Shoes was a poor, ragged, orphan girl named Margery who only had one shoe. Upon being given a full pair she went around showing them off to everyone. With her two shoes, Margery goes around trying to do as much good as possible, and consequently grows up to be comfortable, well off, and happy, thus proving the superiority of a good little girl over "such wicked Folks, who love nothing but Money, and are proud and despise the Poor, and never come to any good in the End." So, from that time on, a *Goody Two Shoes*, (sometimes shortened to *a goody-goody*) is a mocking reference to a woman or girl you think is too smug and self-righteous.

While the tale is no longer in print, the framework of the story has been borrowed by British pantomime—a comedic and musical stage production—and is a regular in the theaters over Christmas time.

Lame duck (noun)

Pitying term for an official or politician who has a title, but no actual power to do anything.

Why *duck*, and why *lame*? No one really knows, but this graphic expression is as common these days in the United States as in the UK. It describes a politician who is still in office but unable, either constitutionally or through waning power, to press his influence and get anything accomplished. The original phrase, however, was not a political reference but a financial one. As far back as the eighteenth century, it was used in the London Stock Market to refer to an investor or broker unable to pay up on settlement day. *Bulls*, *bears*, and *lame ducks* are all financial market metaphors of that period that have survived to the present day.

Lollipop man (noun)

Affectionate term for the patrol person who helps children to cross the road outside school and carries a stop sign resembling a giant lollipop.

Lollipop is the common name for what is officially called the School Crossing Patrol Service, set up in the 1950s to assist young children in crossing the road on the way to or from school. First established by the police, and maintained later by local councils, the patrols have legal powers under the Road Traffic Act of 1984, and car drivers are required by law to respect the patrol and to stop when told.

The pet name for the organization derives from the large round STOP signs carried by the men and women, which, to some, resemble a lollipop. Many children grow up with good memories of the cheery smile of the lollipop man (or lollipop lady) helping them across the road, an image of security and safety. The very term *lollipop* is a positive one for children, as lollipops are considered to be special treats.

But all is not well in lollipop land. There are increasing instances of intimidation and aggression from members of the public and, in 2007, more than fourteen hundred patrols were assaulted, with many of the victims needing hospital treatment. It appears that nowadays, drivers and others resent the demand to stop—a sad symptom of the impatience and haste of modern life.

Maiden aunt (noun)

A somewhat severe unmarried aunt or old maid who is busy serving the community and stands for no nonsense.

For sociological reasons that are hard to pin down, the middle class families of Britain often have at least one unmarried (maiden) aunt.

These ladies are formidable members of society, using their energy in many public-spirited ways. They are usually committed churchgoers and they dress in robust, sensible clothing—tweed skirts and flat shoes being preferred. With their steely hairdos and sometimes brisk manner, they can come across as rather severe. Embracing children is not something that they usually do. Indeed, a certain maiden aunt of my acquaintance used to greet me with arm stretched out as far as it would go, making it clear that no intimacy was even to be entertained.

In a famous speech given in 1993, then Prime Minister John Major was reported as saying, "Fifty years on from now, Britain will still be the country of long shadows on county [cricket] grounds, warm beer, invincible green suburbs, dog lovers, and old maids bicycling to Holy Communion through the morning mist." The original description of the bicycling maiden aunts comes from the essay "England Your England" by George Orwell, an enthusiast for all things English and traditional. According to these two sources, the maiden aunt is sewn into the very fabric of English society and will continue to be so for many years.

Nowt so queer as folk (expression)

A saying that remarks kindly on the foibles and strangeness of other people, and roughly translates as "Human beings are a funny bunch."

A recent antidote to the complicated world we live in has been found in the robust cheerfulness of many northern-English people. As the subject of a number of popular movies and TV series, they have displayed a strong sense of community, straightforward speech, a sense of humor, and a philosophy of keeping your feet on the ground. All these have clearly resonated with Americans, too. What could be clearer then, than the saying, *Nowt so queer as folk*, a typical utterance which, to be convincing, has to be spoken with a rich northern Yorkshire or Lancashire accent.

But first a little explanation. There is no sexual reference in this, it simply states the obvious, but frequently forgotten truth that there's nothing so strange as people. And while we're on the subject, a moment to reflect on the classic northern observation that "All the world's mad save thee and me; and even thee's a little queer."

OAP (noun phrase)

Old age pensioner. A person over sixty-five who believes that everything was better in the olden days.

Official figures show that the UK's population is aging, and that Old Age Pensioners (OAPs) are slowly but surely taking over the country. In the last thirty-five years, the population over the age of sixty-five grew by thirty-one percent—from 7.4 to 9.7 million—against a general population rise of eight percent. Indeed, the largest percentage growth in population in the year to mid-2006 was at ages eighty-five and over (5.9 percent), reaching a record 1.2 million.

OAPs don't always age gracefully. "I don't believe it," is the impatient cry of aging suburbanite Victor Meldrew, comic hero of the TV comedy series *One Foot in the Grave*. And what doesn't he believe? Usually some irritating aspect of the modern world with which he hasn't quite connected. In a society that has undergone bewildering change in the last fifty years, *Grumpy Old Men* (GOMs) like Victor abound. They can't quite see the point of much that passes for standard in the twenty-first century, and have unshakable faith in the theory that everything, yes, everything, was once better than it is today.

OAPs all over the country were delighted in 1992 when they got their own monthly magazine, *The Oldie*. To see if you qualify as a true oldie yourself, and therefore as a potential reader of the magazine, you are invited to answer twenty questions, including: When you hear of *Big Brother*, do you still think of George Orwell? Do you refer to *the wireless*? Do you save string? Can you waltz? Are you obsessively concerned about the size and shape of spoons? Do you know what a pronoun is?

Old school tie (noun phrase)

A term used to denote membership of a group of people who went to the same exclusive school.

George Bernard Shaw once wrote, "It is impossible for an Englishman to open his mouth without making some other

Englishman hate him." Although some would have us believe that the British class system is dead and buried, a different story is told by the huge number of judgmental words used to describe British people who are perceived to be of a different class to the speaker. The old school tie connection is a case in point—a reference to the practice of members of the upper classes showing favor to others simply because they went to the *right* school, that is, a very expensive one, and, more often than not, the same school as they did.

People like us (noun phrase)

Used by people of the right social set or family background to indicate that they approve of, and belong to, the right crowd.

Often abbreviated to PLU, this phrase originates in the 1940s milieu typified by the artistic, wayward, and eccentric Mitford sisters, daughters of the second Baron Redesdale. We get a flavor of the attitude when Nancy Mitford, in an August 1957 letter to her sister Jessica, declared, "People Like Us are never killed in earthquakes."

Nancy refined the art of social class distinctions in her book *Noblesse Oblige* with a list of subtle differences in vocabulary first defined as *U and non-U* by the sociolinguist Alan Ross in 1954. For *U* openers, we have *napkin, bike, rich, jam,* and *lavatory*; while *non-U* gives us: *serviette, cycle, wealthy,*

preserve, and *toilet*. These may seem arbitrary, but they bear out
the daily truth that your speech betrays your social standing.
In reality, of course, U people will instantly identify your place
in society by your shoes or the cut of your clothes. Similarly, in
a famous put-down, a Tory grandee once said of a self-made
colleague, "He bought all his own furniture"—implying that
anyone of class would naturally inherit such things.

Posh (adjective)

*Often used by the lower social classes to describe a person with money
and a privileged background.*

The original use of the term *posh* referred to the position of
ship's cabins on the long sea journey out to India in the days
of the Raj. *Port-Out; Starboard-Home* was the preferred location
as those sides of the ship suffered less from the heat of direct
sunlight on the corresponding journey. Naturally, passengers
with more social importance and higher incomes booked the
preferred cabins.

The term came into more general use to describe anyone
with money and a certain social background, both attributes
being required to qualify for the label. Only the genuine social
article was *posh*, the newly rich being considered a lesser and
more vulgar breed.

The truly posh rose effortlessly to become members of
government and captains of industry, mostly through the **old
school tie** network and then a typical Oxford and Cambridge
education, where relationships with their own kind were forged
for life (see **Oxbridge**). Among so-called public schools (in
reality, expensive and private), centuries-old institutions such

as Eton, Harrow, and Winchester continue to represent the most select places for educating and preparing youngsters for the hardships of wealthy adulthood.

It need hardly be said that the privileged upper classes do not use the term *posh* themselves. *Posh* was always how the lower social classes saw both them and their lifestyle, thus conveying a strange mixture of resentment, envy, and admiration. A posh car, residence, suit, hotel, accent, school— all of these might be uttered with appreciation rather than disgust, as labels of quality, not inequality.

The twentieth century, of course, saw a great social leveling, and the last fifty years especially have witnessed the growing realization in England of the American dream—that anyone from any background can become anything they want. But no matter how rich and important you might rise to be, you can never *become* posh. The distinction persists in British society to this day though the influence of the posh class has dramatically waned.

Nonetheless, history is a cyclical business, and an article in the *Daily Telegraph* asks the question "Has the time come when it's cool to be posh?" Writing about the recent resurgence of old Etonians in politics, Neil Tweedie detects a *New Posh* rising in English public life, as opposed to *Stuffy Old Posh*. He speculates, "The current liking for, or at least tolerance of, poshness may be a reaction to the uglier aspects of the money culture that has dominated the last two decades." We shall just have to see, then, what kind of brave future lies ahead, into which postmodern *New Posh* could lead us. (See also **toff**)

Toff (noun)

*A derisive term for a person with more money than sense. Similar to someone who is **posh**, but usually more ridiculous.*

Class distinction is alive and well in England, and though perhaps the battling socialist years of class warfare are behind us, it may still be the case, as the 2008 *Rough Guide to England* suggests that, "we are obsessed with toffs." So it is not that surprising to hear, as occurred in a recent local election, a Labour candidate accusing his Conservative opponent of being a Tory toff, that is, a Conservative of wealth and position.

The *Oxford English Dictionary* places the origin of the word *toff* as a corruption of *tuft*, the gold tassel once worn by titled undergraduates at Oxford and Cambridge.

To be sure, the label *toff* is not intended to be a kind one. The suggestion is of someone far removed from the concerns and trials of ordinary people. After all, to be a real toff is to be of privileged birth, elegantly dressed, careless with wealth, and probably inclined toward boisterous behavior when out drinking with fellow toffs.

Few of these qualities would attract the average voter, you would imagine. But who knows? For the so-called Tory toff won the election.

Twitcher (noun)

A person who inhabits the countryside spending hours on end hoping to catch sight of a rare bird. Comes with binoculars.

Scientifically known as ornithology, birdwatching is far too serious to be called a hobby. It requires enormous patience, as well as the endurance to be very still and quiet for long periods of time. Having all these qualities, unlike their Continental cousins, the British are perfectly suited to birdwatching. Any sighting of a small brown bird might just be the rare Newfoundland lark that has been blown across the Atlantic and has landed in Cornwall for the first time ever. Once a rarity has been seen, hundreds of twitchers—that is, truly fanatical birdwatchers—rush to the place with their binoculars in hope of catching a glimpse of their quarry.

WAGs (noun phrase)

A frankly silly acronym and phrase coined by newspaper copy editors to describe the pampered wives and girlfriends of rich soccer players.

On the subject of acronyms and abbreviated phrases, newspaper copy editors have contributed a lot to shaping our language into short, witty headlines and to creating new meanings at the same time. Once we thought we knew what a *wag* was: someone who liked telling funny stories. But now WAGs are wives and girlfriends, usually of millionaire soccer players. These charming companions of sporting heroes turn up to major events as if on a fashion parade. Some are already famous in their own right, like ex-Spice Girl Victoria Beckham, or Cheryl Cole of the group Girls Aloud. Others have been plucked from relative obscurity where they worked as waitresses, personal trainers, or beauticians. Now they compete for the attention of the cameras in their designer clothes, flashing (mainly) fake tans and $50,000 diamond accessories. All of those assets, plus a strong, handsome man with a luxury pad in Liverpool, Cheshire, or Mayfair, should be enough to make any girl smile when the photographers call for it.

Warts and all (expression)

Describes a person whose ugliness is not covered over but in plain view.

Some of the contradictions of the English character are nicely summed up by the "Royalists and Roundheads" opposition of the seventeenth century during the English Civil War. On the one hand, the love of ceremony, decoration, and pomp that goes with our royal family; on the other, a very different kind of modesty and realism that may stem from a long Protestant heritage. This saying goes back to a time when portraits of the great and good were usually painted with some discretion, the main object being to disguise the less attractive features of the sitter. This would always have been the case with royal portraits. But when the new Lord Protector, Oliver Cromwell (the Puritan parliamentarian who overthrew King Charles I) was having his portrait done around 1657, he insisted that the artist, Sir Peter Lely, should not flatter him at all, but show "all the roughness, pimples, warts, and everything as you see me, otherwise I will never pay you a farthing for it." So it was to be, with the portrait we now have in the Bolton Art Gallery showing a large wart below Cromwell's mouth.

Wellies (Wellington boots) (noun)

Practical but unlovely waterproof rubber boots and the go-to footwear for country Brits.

The Duke of Wellington was the first to take the standard so-called Hessian boot, fashionable for the military in the eighteenth century, and redesign it to his own taste. What he came up with was thereafter known as the Wellington boot, a soft leather, mid-calf design that was both practical for day wear and comfortable enough for evenings in the field.

What we have now come to call wellies are a tough, PVC, waterproof version of the Duke's boots, suitable for walking over wet and muddy ground, and standard wear for country dwellers. *Green wellies* is a slightly mocking term for those middle and upper class *weekender* country folk who disdain the normal black color used by people actually working on the land.

White van man (noun)

The driver of a small van often criticized by the general populace for his aggressive driving style, yet in reality no worse than other drivers on British roads.

If an Englishman's home is his castle, then his car is his forward mobile gun position. For the enemy is out there on the roads, too, and we must be prepared. This attitude is said to explain the popularity of *four by fours*, high-fuel-consumption vehicles built like tanks and often reinforced with serious looking cow fenders. Such vehicles are built to cross deserts and mountain ranges, but in practice rarely go farther than the school gates or the local shopping mall.

So who, exactly, is the enemy here? They include boy racers, men in cloth caps, and the most studied of all, the White Van Man, driver of a small van, which typically is white and unlabeled. Sarah Kennedy, a BBC radio presenter, is credited with identifying WVM in the late 1990s. He exists mainly as a stereotype, by nature guilty of aggressive and inconsiderate driving—cutting off, pulling out, tailgating, and generally in a hurry at the expense of every other driver. We have all experienced WVM, but does he really exist as a type?

A survey from the Oxford-based Social Issues Research concludes that, yes, the image does reflect the reality in a small fraction of cases, but that most of the 2.5 million white van drivers in the country are no worse than any other category of driver. Still, we have to have someone to hate, don't we? I'm presently conducting a personal survey of BMW man on the roads.

Yob (noun)

A pejorative, informal term for a working-class person who behaves in a loutish or antisocial way. Natural enemy of the **toff**.

First recorded in the early 1920s, the term *yob* is derived from English back slang for boy—a way of speaking in code by spelling words backward that was popular at the time.

Yob originally referred to a working-class boy but has evolved into a term for a general hooligan, lout, or uncouth youth. Rude, noisy, and aggressive, he (or she) specializes in drunken, antisocial behavior of the worst kind.

What can be done to restore the traditional good manners of the British social order? In the late 1990s, Prime Minister Tony Blair introduced the antisocial behavior order (ASBO) for offenses including swearing, drinking, and causing a public nuisance. Inevitably, its introduction caused something of a scandal, in part because it was a clear indication of the deterioration of general social respect. The ASBO is being withdrawn, but the word remains as *yobs* can also be referred to as *asbos*.

The *yob* is closely related to the *chav*, who is a flashier version, prone to displays of jewelry and certain designer brands. If you're still having trouble picturing these terms, think trailer trash in the US, or *bogan* in Australia.

The King's English

In times gone by, it was essential to know the **King's English** in order to be accepted in British society. The rules have relaxed, though, and you won't lose your head if you make a mistake! However, you still need to make the right impression when visiting Britain, so remember to use phrases like **Bob's your uncle** and **thingamabob**, with a lot of **umming and erring** in between. Here's everything you need to know **in a nutshell**.

All mouth and no trousers (expression)

Used to describe a man whose sense of self-importance is in inverse proportion to his actual relevance.

This expression is well known in the north of England as a woman's crushing remark about any man with oversized ideas about himself. *Mouth* refers to "brash talk," and *trousers* to the British term for pants. The grammarian's term for such a phrase, where the container stands for the thing contained, is *metonymy*. What is interesting in this case is the implication that trousers in themselves, or rather, the men inside them, have a negative quality. One might have thought that such a feminist attitude is a modern invention, but far from it. The robust women of the north have long been conducting their own battle with male chauvinism.

However, through being adopted more widely in England—possibly via the influence of TV programs based in the north—the phrase has gone through a curious transformation, through a process known to linguists as *spontaneous change*. The obvious negative of "trousers" has corrupted the expression into "all mouth and no trousers," a form in which it now frequently appears. This may have come about by false analogy with similar phrases such as, "all talk and no action," "all bread and no cheese," and "all bark and no bite." What is amusing here, is that the corrupted version of the saying has unwittingly restored a positive value to trousers.

As pleased as Punch (expression)

To be very pleased indeed. Named after a wicked puppet that was popular with children in years gone by and who delighted in his own bad behavior.

People of a certain age will remember the childish pleasures of summertime in fairs and days at the beach that often included the Punch and Judy puppet show. The appallingly wicked behavior of Mr. Punch, who beat all around him with his stick, would raise shrieks of laughter, matched only by the squeals when a crocodile popped up with its terrible jaws. The association with *as pleased as* arose from the fact that the grotesque figure of Punch wore a permanent grin and is delighted with his own wickedness, crying "That's the way to do it!" after each of his foul deeds. It is not recorded if children who grew up watching this puppet show went on to become violent adults, but my guess would be that the whole thing was fairly harmless.

The tradition of the violent puppet show goes way back, at least to the seventeenth century, originating in the Italian puppet shows of *Punchinello*, or *Polichinello*, which were popular across all of Europe. The entertainment seems to have come to England around 1662, when we find the

London diarist Samuel Pepys noting a repeat visit to a show which, "pleased me mightily." Modern political correctness has dealt a severe blow to this kind of diversion, but the phrase endures.

At sixes and sevens (expression)

In a state of disarray and confusion, not necessarily resulting from a mathematical conundrum.

Personally I am all at sixes and sevens about this saying because nobody seems to have a clear idea of where it comes from. The favorite approximation comes from Chaucer's *Troilus and Criseyde*, around 1375, where he writes "to set the world on six and seven." Two centuries later, in *Richard II*, Shakespeare has the Duke of York saying "All is uneven, And everything is left at six and seven." By the eighteenth century dictionaries had arrived at the present form of *at sixes and sevens*.

Theorists have leaped at any combination of six and seven in literature, from the Bible onward, to find some consistent root for the saying. After long research, I can only conclude that the real basis of the saying comes from modern author Douglas Adams's revelation that the answer to the mystery of life, the Universe, and everything, is forty-two, namely, seven sixes, or six sevens, however you want to see it. Scientists, including the great Richard Feynman, have demonstrated the extraordinary presence of the number forty-two in cosmic mathematics.

This is so utterly puzzling that it must leave all of us at sixes and sevens.

Baker's dozen (noun phrase)

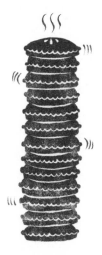

Another way of counting thirteen.

Whereas a normal dozen is twelve, a baker's dozen is thirteen, and for the following reason. Selling short weight is an age-old practice and most ancient civilizations imposed standard weights and measures in order to make regular and reliable trade possible. The Romans in particular established their own standards in Britain, which lasted for centuries after they had gone. Pounds, ounces, pence, and miles all originated in Roman measures, though many Saxon standards were kept in use as well, especially for land ownership.

For day-to-day trading purposes, medieval guilds maintained their own standards and ensured their traders honored them. One basic product that lent itself to cheating was bread, as it can be hard to make loaves of a consistent size and weight. So at least as early as the thirteenth century the bakers' guild, the Worshipful Company of Bakers, introduced the practice of adding a little extra *in-bread* to the loaf sold, in order to ensure they were not selling underweight, for which the punishment was severe. For the same reason, when selling bread in bulk to other traders, they added a thirteenth loaf to every twelve sold. Thus, thirteen loaves became known as a *baker's dozen*.

Bob's your uncle (expression)

A nonsensical saying meaning "and there you are!" or "It's that simple!"

This phrase refers to any task that can be accomplished neatly and simply with a kind of precision, after which one can say with satisfaction "and Bob's your uncle." The expression naturally lends itself to all sorts of silly and disbelieving replies, such as, "and Fanny's my aunt."

It supposedly originated with the appointment of Arthur Balfour, nephew of the Victorian Prime Minister Robert Cecil, Lord Salisbury, to be Chief Secretary for Ireland in 1887, an office for which no one, other than his Uncle Robert, thought he had any useful qualifications at all. So he got the job purely because Bob was his uncle. A nice theory, and no one has come up with anything convincingly better.

Bowdlerize (verb)

To edit a literary work in a prudish manner, reflecting Victorian values. Needless to say, rarely seen nowadays.

Thomas Bowdler (1754–1825) had retired from being a doctor and clearly had nothing better to do so he decided to edit the works of Shakespeare to make them more *suitable* for family reading.

His *Family Shakespeare* appeared in 1807 with the necessary cuts, including the deletion of entire characters whom he deemed altogether too bawdy. This prudish kind of editing has since been known as *bowdlerizing*, arising out of the strict morality that is generally referred to as *Victorian values*.

The tendency nowadays is to go to the other extreme and tease every sexual reference, whether intended or not, out of classic costume dramas. Both the nineteenth-century novelists Mrs. Gaskell and Jane Austen have undergone these influences in TV adaptations, to the horror of literary purists.

By hook or by crook (expression)

A very old phrase meaning to use any means possible and bearing no relation to criminals.

It is good to find a phrase in common use that goes back as far as this one, and that appears (though not entirely proven) to connect us to our feudal past. The first recorded use of the phrase is from the fourteenth century.

In medieval times when the peasantry were not allowed to cut down trees, they were permitted nonetheless to gather firewood from loose or dead branches that could be obtained using a *hook* (bill-hook) or a *crook*, a staff with a curved end like the kind shepherds would use. No doubt desperate peasants often exceeded the strict use of these tools, and so the term has evolved into its current usage meaning to achieve something by whatever means possible. Some aspects of human nature certainly remain unchanged.

By Jingo (expression)

A saying that arose from the gloating nationalism that
was common among Brits when Britannia ruled the waves.

This term, nodding to a rather aggressive and overconfident nationalism, takes us right back to our imperial days again, when Britain ruled the waves and a lot more besides. A long-standing threat to our interests throughout the nineteenth century, Russia moved into the Balkans in an expansionist gesture against Turkey and upset us mightily. As a result, the major European powers summoned both sides to the Congress of Berlin in 1878 and worked out a settlement, as the diplomats say, to restore stability. What this really means, of course, is carving up the world to suit ourselves and our allies, in this case the Austro–Hungarian dynasty of the Hapsburgs who were terrified of Slavic nationalism rearing its head.

A popular song of the time had already raised spirits at home, and a phrase in its rousing chorus became a byword for imperialistic gloating over the forthcoming challenge to Russia:

> *We don't want to fight but by Jingo if we do*
> *We've got the ships, we've got the men, we've got the money too*
> *We've fought the Bear before, and while we're Britons true*
> *The Russians shall not have Constantinople.*

Up to this time, *by Jingo* was no more than one of the many euphemisms for *by God* or *by Jesus* in popular language, but now found its new form of *jingoes*, or warmongers, in a letter from the campaigning socialist G. J. Holyoake to the radical London newspaper, the *Daily News*.

Crumbs! (exclamation)

An expression that is used innocently by children to mean "Goodness!" It is closely related to other jolly British terms like "Golly Gosh!" and "Cor blimey!"

British children who grew up on literature featuring schoolboy heroes like Bunter, William, and Jennings, let alone the manifold works of Enid Blyton, will instantly recognize the strength of emotion that can go into a simple exclamation like *Crumbs!*

Yet despite its seemingly childish innocence, this term, along with its cousin *Crikey!*, is a euphemism for Christ, which in more respectful times was a taboo utterance, at least when said profanely.

Related, though perhaps slightly less innocent, is the exclamation *Cor blimey!*—often shortened to just *Cor!* This phrase is a version of *Gor blimey!* which itself is a verbal turn on the exclamation "God blind me!" Like *Crumbs!* it can express either surprise or anger.

Dog and bone (noun)

A phrase used in Cockney rhyming slang to mean a telephone.

You would never guess that this means a phone. This creative style of speech is a peculiarity of Cockneys, those born within the sound of Bow Bells, namely the bells of St. Mary-le-Bow church in Cheapside in the City of London. They have a long renown as witty and enterprising street traders, and more recently as financial market traders. These folk invented a way of substituting words for others that rhymed, calling stairs for example, *apples and pears*. A hat is known as a *titfer* (short for *tit-for-tat*). The special feature of rhyming slang is that the rhyme comes from a pair of words, but only the first word is

used as an abbreviation. So a phone (*dog and bone*) is referred to as a *dog*. A suit (*whistle and flute*) is a *whistle*. Put them altogether, and a hatless man on his way out to the local pub might ask his *trouble* to be a dear and pop up the *apples* for his *titfer*. Translated: Our gent is asking his wife (*trouble and strife*) to pop up the stairs (*apples*) and bring him his hat. See? It's easy when you know how! Here are some other well-known examples of Cockney rhyming slang:

Brown bread: dead

Butcher's hook: have a look

China plate: mate

Mincers (shortened from *mince pies*): eyes

Plates (shortened from *plates of meat*): feet

Feather in your cap (noun phrase)

A crowning achievement of which one is especially proud.

It would be a pity not to include at least one reference to our chivalric past. The expression a *feather in your cap* originally dates to medieval times when knights were honored for their bravery on the field with plumes to wear on their helmets.

The best known example of this has to be the Prince of Wales's Feathers—the three ostrich feathers bestowed on the Black Prince after the Battle of Crécy in 1346, and now the principal emblem of the badge of the heir to the British throne. The three feathers can be seen on the current two-pence coin in Britain as well.

Feathers continue to have a symbolic place in heraldry—the right to wear them usually being the privilege of those with certain offices or honors. A number of inns and pubs also bear the name *The Feathers*, in recognition of the royal coat of arms.

Flummox (verb)

One is flummoxed if one is lost for answers or stumped.

The origin of the word *flummox* is in itself flummoxing; no one knows where this word comes from, not even *The Oxford English Dictionary*.

A dialectal term, first recorded in the nineteenth century, *flummox* means to puzzle or confuse. But we can imagine it on the lips of a countryman in some rural British setting, staring at the horizon as he tries to figure out the meaning to some deep question, and eventually comes out with "Well, that's got me right flummoxed!"

Gobsmacked (adjective)

Lost for words, speechless.

This wonderful term comes from joining two delightfully incorrect slang words: *gob*, a not very polite Celtic slang word for "mouth," and *smacked*, meaning "to hit," as in a related phrase, "smacked in the kisser." But no violence is intended in *gobsmacked*, which simply means "left speechless"—though this may have the same effect as being smacked in the kisser.

Gobsmacked came to public fame on the lips of a leading Conservative politician, Chris Patten, a member of Mrs. Thatcher's administration, who liked to descend from the heights of his classical education and speak the language of the people. *Double whammy* (double blow) and *porkies* (pork pies = lies, in Cockney rhyming slang) were other colorful terms he used. Whether because of, or in spite of, the irritation caused by such talk, Patten lost his parliamentary seat in the 1992 election and went off to annoy the Chinese as the last Governor of Hong Kong.

How's your father? (expression)

A somewhat bawdy term for bedroom activities, traditionally unmentionable by name in British households.

Yet another slang expression for sexual activity, this is a twentieth-century phrase, probably originating with the music-hall comedian Harry Tate (1872–1940), who would use it to change the subject whenever a conversation took a difficult turn. From this, it came into general use for anything a speaker did not wish to name, and then, inevitably, as sex was so often the unnamed subject, it found its home in expressions like having a bit of *how's-your-father* (see also **"it"**). In a spoof etymology, the phrase comes from the practice of Victorian fathers hiding under their daughters' voluminous skirts in order to protect her virtue so that a panting suitor would always carefully ask, "How's your father?" before lurching into the arms of his beloved.

I'm a Dutchman (expression)

A mocking term based on a long history of dislike of foreigners; in particular, the Dutch.

Partly because of our insular character, but also partly because of our history of aggressively roaming the world, the English have a rich variety of abusive terms for foreigners. And we reserve special contempt for other Europeans who, at various times, have competed with us for power. It is hard to imagine now, but the Dutch were once the special object of our loathing and contempt, probably because their seafaring skills were once equal to ours. Indeed, we borrowed a wide range of sailing words from the Dutch language, including *skipper*, *landlubber*, *boom*, *hull*, and *sloop*.

In 1667, during the Anglo–Dutch wars of the seventeenth century, a Dutch fleet sailed up the Medway River and did much damage to our ships and defenses. To add insult, they even towed away an English flagship. A wave of anti-Dutch sentiment swept London, and pamphlets and news-sheets all had their day in ridiculing the Netherlandish people as "a nation of cheese-mongers and herring-picklers, muddy and greedy," as Henry Hitchings writes. The strength of feeling is shown by how many negative terms based around the Dutch survive to this day. Terms like *bumpkin* and *nitwit* came from the Dutch language to describe their national character. Expressions like *Dutch courage*, *Dutch auction*, and similar phrases played on the notion of insincerity and falsehood. All of this culminated with the phrase at hand, the ultimate insult of all, used today in statements like, "These pies are the best in town, and if you find better then *I'm a Dutchman*."

Much ill-feeling between the two nations was laid to rest in 1688 when William of Orange, Protestant nephew of Charles II and James II, landed in England to assume the throne, prevent another English Civil War, and form an alliance that would contain the rising French influence under the Sun King, Louis XIV.

In a nutshell (adverbial phrase)

A Shakespearean phrase meaning to pack a lot into a small space, or to summarize.

"Oh God, I could be bounded in a nutshell and count myself a King of infinite space," cries Hamlet in Shakespeare's tragic play. But the meaning of the modern expression goes way back to classical times where, in his *Natural History,* Pliny writes, "Cicero records that a parchment copy of Homer's poem *The Iliad* was enclosed *in a nutshell* (*in nuce*)."

In Shakespeare's own time, a Bible is said to have been produced that could fit into a nutshell, and that curiosity may have come to the playwright's notice before he adopted the phrase as his own.

In a pretty pickle (adverbial phrase)

Another food-related phrase meaning to be in a bit of trouble, similar to being "in a stew."

Another phrase found in Shakespeare, this time on the lips of Trinculo in *The Tempest,* "I have been in such a pickle since I saw you last." The phrase was already in existence, borrowed from the Dutch expression *to sit in a pickle*—pickle being the salt brine used for preserving meat or fish, so really not a very pleasant place to be.

With time, a nice English ironic twist to the phrase became *in a pretty pickle,* thus typically understating the experience of being in an unpleasant, embarrassing, or awkward situation.

"To be in a stew" is another common food metaphor, here with the meaning of being in trouble or rage over a bad situation. The term *stew* at different times in its history has meant the cooking pot itself (compare *stove* from the same Old French origin), the food cooked in it, hot bath houses (*stews*), and from that, houses of ill repute. Any of these sounds like a most undesirable place to be getting hot under the collar.

(The) King's English (noun)

Title of the classic book on English usage and grammar written by brothers Henry and Francis Fowler in 1906.

The King's English, written by brothers H. W. and F. G. Fowler, is a classic description and robust defense of our language as it should be, according to the rules of grammar and good style. With its stern commentaries on everything from unattached participles to trite phrases and cheap originality, it has been a standard reference work and it is cited whenever ammunition is needed to ridicule any writer's grammatical blunder or inelegance.

This die-hard approach to such matters has softened considerably in recent times, as linguists have come to find positive virtues in English *as she is spoke*, without being constrained by the rule book. So it is with whimsical interest, rather than mischievous intent, that we look at its section on *Americanisms*, which opens thus:

> *Americanisms are foreign words, and should be so treated. To say this is not to insult the American language. It must be recognized*

*that they and we, in parting some hundreds of years ago, started
on slightly divergent roads in language long before we did so in
politics.*

The Fowler brothers' severe conclusion is that "The English
and the American language and literature are both good things;
but they are better apart than mixed." Before moving on, they
open fire on "the barbaric taste illustrated by such town names
as Memphis," not to mention "Emerson's curious bizarre style."

Such blows must still hurt, because although the Fowlers'
broadside is now a hundred years
old, Bill Bryson has been moved
to reply in equally robust but
slightly over-sensitive terms that
"without America's contribution,
English today would enjoy a
global importance about on
a par with Portuguese." With
some inconsistency, he points
out how much British English
has absorbed *Americanisms,* but
then concludes how much room
there remains for misunderstanding
each other. As Oscar Wilde put it neatly
in his short story *The Canterville Ghost,*
"We have really everything in common
with America nowadays except, of course,
language."

Kiss me, Hardy (expression)

Reputedly the last words of admiral Lord Nelson, head of the English fleet during the Napoleonic Wars.

Much discussion has been generated over the years by this odd little phrase, which was supposed to be the last utterance of our national hero, Lord Nelson, to Captain Thomas Hardy. Nelson was mortally wounded by a musket ball in the final hours of the Battle of Trafalgar when, in one of the most decisive engagements of the Napoleonic wars, the English fleet defeated the Spanish and French naval forces off the southwest coast of Spain.

Some, determined that Nelson would never have said anything so **soppy** to another man, have argued that what he really said was, "Kismet, Hardy," referring to fate or destiny. However, accounts given by eyewitnesses of the event do confirm that Hardy kissed him, a quite normal and unambiguous gesture of friendship between men at the time.

Load of cobblers (noun phrase)

Colorful slang meaning a lot of rubbish or nonsense. Definitely not suitable for use in polite company.

Another of these elusive phrases with their origin in rhyming slang, but I would guess that in this very popular saying most people don't actually know the key word. "A load of cobbler's awls" is the full phrase, in this case *awls* to rhyme with *balls*, which probably needs no further explanation.

Mad as a March hare (expression)

Reflects the traditional association between March hares and madness, amusingly depicted in the children's book Alice in Wonderland.

Hares are beautiful and elegant creatures, but they indulge in eccentric and quite wild behavior during their breeding season over the spring and summer. They appear to have boxing matches with one another, jump in the air, and do other odd antics, giving the impression of a degree of madness.

The expression *mad as a March hare* goes back hundreds of years, and is found in Chaucer's "Friar's Tale" from the fourteenth century.

Both hares and hatters were associated with madness, the latter supposedly suffering because of the poisoning effect of the mercury they used in their craft. In one of the most hilarious scenes in children's literature, Lewis Carroll's Alice comes across both the March Hare and the Mad Hatter having a tea party with a dormouse that they end up shoving into a teapot. Mad indeed!

Mmm (interjection)

One of those conversational enigmas that can mean almost anything and frequently has more "mmms" added to it to make it even more baffling.

Those familiar with British conversation will recognize this common reply to a question, while feeling that its meaning is never quite clear. This is because it can actually have one or even two of several meanings, depending on intonation and gesture (which may be no more than a movement of the eyebrows). It can mean *Yes, No, Maybe, Rather not, Don't think so, Sometimes, Oh, yes? Really?,* or *What do you mean?* A shake or nod of the head will sometimes tell you if the general meaning is positive or negative. The longer *Mmm,* as in *Mmmmmm,* can be taken as indicating severe doubt or reservation. (See **umming and erring**)

Mockney (noun)

A combining of the words mock and cockney, a way of speaking that is a form of reverse snobbery and is designed to disguise any knowledge of the proper way to speak English.

One of the supposed revolutions in modern British life has been the so-called *social leveling* of the classes, a development that arises from the political principle of equal opportunities for all. This is such a radical notion that we had to learn it from our breakaway American colony rather than figure it out for ourselves. But it does seem that we are making our way there, if slowly. One sign of the times is a kind of reverse snobbery that makes it unfashionable to be upper class, and trendy to have what Rudyard Kipling called "the common touch." While a generation ago, young people shed their regional accents in order to get ahead in the world, now they deliberately hide their *received pronunciation* (sometimes called BBC English) and put on an East London, county of Essex, style of speech, more associated with street traders than with aristocratic halls. Phonetics experts will tell you more about this than I have space for, but a key feature of this stylized pronunciation is the *glottal stop*, which involves an arrested breath at the back of the palate instead of a completely enunciated voiceless prepalatal occlusive, e.g., pronouncing Britain as "Bri-in" with the t-sound coming from the back of the throat rather than the tongue and front teeth. Such mockney is seen as a way of mingling with people of all classes without appearing threateningly superior with your accent. As we'll see later, even the Queen herself has been persuaded to join in. (See **Queen's speech**)

Mrs. Malaprop (noun)

The inspiration for the term malapropism.

"Killing's the matter!" exclaims Mrs. Malaprop, a character in Richard Sheridan's 1775 play, *The Rivals*. "—But he can tell you the perpendiculars." By which, of course, she meant the *particulars*.

Mrs. Malaprop has given her name to malapropisms, a classic kind of linguistic error explored and condemned in H. W. and F. G. Fowler's *The King's English*. It arises from trying to sound educated by using a long word, but mistakenly substituting another that sounds like the one you really want.

There are hilarious *malapropisms* from all over the world (even some known as *Bushisms*), but some of the funniest come from the mouth of Mrs. Malaprop herself. Here is a small flavor, with what she really meant in parentheses:

"Sure, if I *reprehend* any thing in this world it is the use of my *oracular* tongue, and a nice *derangement* of *epitaphs*!" (apprehend, vernacular, arrangement, epithets)

"She's as headstrong as an *allegory* on the banks of Nile." (alligator)

"I am sorry to say, Sir Anthony, that my *affluence* over my niece is very small." (influence)

"Oh! it gives me the *hydrostatics* to such a degree." (hysterics)

Naff (adjective)

Uncool or lacking style in a way that is uniquely British and frequently eccentric.

It is hard to imagine that a prime minister's underpants could become the focus of national attention, but that very misfortune befell John Major soon after his arrival at Downing Street in 1990. A TV news image of his clothes in slight disarray revealed that he wore his shirt inside his underwear, instead of tucked between his underwear and his pants.

One possibly has to have been at a boys' boarding school to appreciate the vital difference between these two arrangements. One is fine and acceptable, the other is incredibly, but laughably, naff. Boys will be boys, though, and for years afterward political commentators and cartoonists mercilessly scorned Major's naffness, depicting him as "Superuselessman," with his briefs worn over his pants, in the style of Superman's red shorts. "He's still a joke," wrote the cartoonist, Steve Bell, years later in 2002, thus proving that naffness is something that is never lived down, no matter how high you rise in public life, nor how many decades pass.

Natter (verb)

To chat away harmlessly—and endlessly—about everything.

There's nothing like a good natter on the phone, and the best natterers of course talk **nineteen to the dozen**. It's a happy little word, probably from *gnatter*, a northern dialect word. Honest in its hint of endless chattering, nonetheless it is forgiving and approving at the same time. So it's yet another of those British terms for little human foibles that make life worth living (see **flutter**).

Nineteen to the dozen (expression)

*When something happens quickly, especially in reference to talking or having a **natter**.*

This phrase is most often used to describe speech patterns, hence, she talked *nineteen to the dozen*. The parallel expression, *ten to the dozen*, is used, illogically, in the same sense. This saying goes back to the eighteenth century, but its origin is unclear. One unconvincing source sometimes quoted comes from the introduction of steam pumps to Cornish mines, where their speed of operation cleared nineteen thousand gallons of water for every twelve bushels of coal burned.

Queen's speech (noun phrase)

Traditional televised message from the Queen to her subjects on Christmas Day.

The relationship between the royal family and television has had a somewhat checkered history. Queen Elizabeth II's reign began with a TV event, as her Coronation in June 1953 was the first major national occasion to be televised. I remember watching it as a child on a tiny black-and-white screen in a neighbor's house, as not everyone had TV in those days. Building on the radio tradition begun by her grandfather, the Queen went on to deliver a television message to the nation every Christmas from 1957 onward. This was a speech read out in a live broadcast as the Queen sat in a chair in front of the camera, and was famous for its stiff formality and the oft repeated phrase, "My husband and I..."

Over the years, advisors encouraged the Queen to relax the style of her presentation and she began to present more of a pictorial record of the year, with her voice as background commentary. We now know from academic studies that the Queen's pronunciation has shifted with time, and is now much closer to a popular accent than the so-called *cut-glass* accent of the upper classes of yore. Jonathan Harrington and colleagues at Macquarie University, Sydney, in their 2000 study, wrote:

> *Our analysis reveals that the Queen's pronunciation of some vowels has been influenced by the standard southern British [SSB] accent of the 1980s, which is more typically associated with speakers younger and lower in the social hierarchy. We conclude that the Queen no longer speaks the Queen's English of the 1950s, although the vowels of the 1980s Christmas message are still clearly set apart from those of an SSB accent.*

In an update, published in the *Journal of Phonetics* from December 2006, the author writes:

> *The changes also reflect the changing class structure over the last fifty years. In the 1950s, there was a much sharper distinction between the classes as well as the accents that typified them. Since then, the class boundaries have become more blurred, and so have the accents. Fifty years ago, the idea that Queen's English could be influenced by cockney would have been unthinkable.*

Red herring (noun)

A false scent or misleading suggestion.

We all know about the *red herring* in the plot of a detective novel, the misleading suggestion of a perpetrator and motive for the crime, to throw us off the scent of the real killer. Red herrings, colored so by the process of salting and smoking, were a cheap form of food in the Middle Ages and had a particularly strong smell. The belief is that because of this they were used to mislead hunting dogs by being dragged across country. From this practice came the meaning of a false scent.

Serendipity (noun)

A happy accident.

Serendipity is a made-up word, meaning the way in which we sometimes make happy, but quite accidental discoveries. The English author Horace Walpole coined it in a letter written in 1754, saying he had based it on a Persian fairy tale called *The Three Princes of Serendip*. He explained that the tale's heroes "were always making discoveries, by accidents and sagacity, of things they were not in quest of." *Serendip* is another form of *Sarandip*, the old Persian name for Sri Lanka. In spite of its exotic origins, the word suggests something of the happily amateur temperament of the British, which always seems to allow space for creativity to arise as if by chance.

Thingamabob (noun)

Describes everything from a hatpin to a hamster and is ideal for use when a word is on the tip of your tongue.

We all need a word to use when we cannot think of, or do not know, the name for something. French has *un truc*, Spanish *un chisme*, German *ein Dingsbums*, and Dutch *dinges* (which has passed into US slang as *dingus*). In English the nameless object is called a *thingamabob*, and sometimes a *thingy* for short, or a *whatchamacallit*, *whatsit*, *whatnot*, or *gizmo*. Armed with these, we need never learn any more vocabulary! "Please pass me the *thingamajig* on the *whatnot*. No, not the red *gizmo*, the *whatsit* with the round *thingy* on the end."

Umming and erring (noun, verb)

Conversational fillers frequently used by a nation of wafflers and essential learning for aspiring Anglophiles.

It's clear that the English love to **natter** on the phone, and a recent report from BT, the British telephone company, revealed that the average UK household spends more than fifty-eight hours on the telephone every year. But the study also showed that about ten percent of that time is made up of pure waffle, what linguists call *filler words*. These exist in most languages but seem especially marked in English speakers, as: *er, um, you know, well, actually, know what I mean?* Psychological expert Phillip Hodson, who carried out the research, comments:

> *This BT study reveals Britain to be a nation of wafflers. The descendants of Shakespeare, the guardians of* The Oxford English Dictionary, *have become lazier conversationalists. Every twenty-four hours, a talker in Britain might use up to ten thousand redundant or filler words, or word repetitions. This amounts to about seven wasted words per minute and only ten seconds pass before we relapse into further waffle.*

Whinge (verb)

To complain or moan.

The British at home really dislike whingers, those who complain endlessly and ineffectually. *Whinge* is derived from *whine*, which has a similar meaning, but more often refers to the sound rather than the content, though both words have their origin in Old English. Here we must bear in mind the stoical nature of the British, the Blitz spirit that, as in the bombing of London in the Second World War, enables us to endure pain and misfortune with something approaching cheerfulness. However, take us away from **Old Blighty** and what happens? We have another reputation altogether, summed up by the Australians' label of *whingeing Poms*.

Fair Play

The Brits are nearly obsessed with good manners. To fit in with polite company it's essential to master time-honored rules like **minding your Ps and Qs**, apologizing frequently, and **queuing** without complaint. As a general rule, remember to be self-effacing and cheerful at all times. Don't be different, don't cause offense, and if all else fails, KEEP CALM AND CARRY ON!

All right (adjectival phrase)

A noncommittal and understated answer to any question.

If there is one thing the British are famous for, it must be understatement. This particular quirk is an endless source of confusion for Americans, who prefer plain speaking or, as in the case of the monosyllabic cowboy, very little speech at all. The habit of understatement is clearly inherited, for if you ask a very small child what their school is like, you will almost certainly get the answer, "All right." This answer cannot possibly have been learned at anyone's knee, and must be an acquired British characteristic passed on genetically, thus disproving Darwinian theory in one stroke.

That same child will go on all through life answering all right to all sorts of questions ranging from, "What was the weather like?" to, we can only suppose, "What did you think of your funeral service?"

Argy-bargy (noun, verb)

Playful word for a disagreement, such as when two men quarrel in a pub.

This funny little term, both noun and verb, refers to a minor quarrel or spat. It is, perhaps, not in such common use as it was and has a more innocent ring to it than what today might be called *aggro*, or aggressive. It is probably a corruption of a Scots phrase *argle-bargle*, which we find in Robert Louis Stevenson's *Kidnapped*. Many popular words have a similar dual structure, a feature of languages all over the world, possibly related to a baby's first attempts to talk. A *word double* can be created either by simply repeating the term (*bye bye, no-no*) or by rhyming with or echoing it (*honey-bunny, dingle-dangle*). The result is fun, expressive, and delightfully creative.

Balderdash (noun)

Similar in meaning to **load of cobblers,** *but a little more polite.*

An exclamation of mysterious origin, but traceable as far back as 1596, this spluttering word originally referred to a jumbled mix of liquors. By 1674 it meant a "senseless collection of words and general nonsense or noise," and in the eighteenth century, entered Samuel Johnson's *Dictionary of the English Language* as "a rude mixture." One may safely draw the conclusion that the educated British mind, with its respect for common sense, order, and logic, has little patience with arguments that are patently nonsense. (See **humbug**)

Blackball (verb)

To ban or bar someone from membership of an exclusive club or institution.

This phrase, meaning to exclude or shun, comes from a background that is quintessentially British, and is intimately linked to our well-established systems of privilege. Traditionally, a certain proof of a gentleman's social standing was the London club or clubs to which he belonged. In the past, these were all male preserves and to join, a candidate had to be proposed by an existing member. The practice was to vote in secret, using a bag into which the members, one by one, placed a colored ball (yes) or a black ball (no). Then the balls were counted. In some institutions, one black ball was sufficient to exclude the candidate, in others it had to be a majority of black balls. Either way, membership was denied and the candidate was blackballed.

English society being what it is, the fact of being blackballed by a club was enough to cast a dark shadow over someone's character. Few would think it likely that the black ball was merely the fruit of another gentleman's meanness, envy, or vindictiveness. Gentlemen don't behave like that, do they?

Curate's egg (noun phrase)

Polite phrase that describes something that is good in parts, but not the whole.

Being diplomatic comes all too easily to the British, and a humorous cartoon of 1895 gave rise to the phrase *a bit of a curate's egg*. A curate (that is, an assistant clergyman) is having breakfast with his bishop and is clearly in trouble as he eats his egg. The bishop says, "I'm afraid you have a bad egg, Mr. Jones," to which the poor man, anxious not to offend his superior, replies, "Oh no, my Lord, I assure you that parts of it are excellent!"

A *curate's egg* is therefore used to refer to something, such as a book being reviewed, which out of politeness one does not wish to condemn utterly. "Like the curate's egg, good in parts" is a common use of the phrase.

Don't mind me! (expression)

Typically British phrase that is confusing for non-Brits because it can be used both as an apology and an admonishment.

One of the most nuanced phrases ever uttered and very revealing of the apparently self-deprecating manners of a British person. Like "**Mmm**," "Tell me about it," and "**With respect**," the true meaning depends entirely on the context. But with such statements, very often the real sense is the opposite of what the words appear to mean. If you hear "Don't mind me!" then you are either listening to a genuine apology from someone for disturbing you, or else being a complete nuisance yourself.

Similarly, "Tell me about it!" is usually uttered as an exclamation meaning, in reality, "I already know this so well, so don't even begin to tell me about it!" Like "You can say that again!" it's certainly not an invitation to repeat what you just said.

Perhaps with phrases like these in mind—commonly used but sometimes perplexing—the 2008 *Rough Guide to England*, authored by four British travel writers, warns overseas visitors that the British are "the most contradictory people imaginable" and comes to the slightly despairing conclusion that, "However long you spend in the country you'll never figure them out."

Elbow grease (noun)

Hard work, not necessarily by using one's elbows but using considerable effort.

This phrase, meaning hard, physical work, goes back to at least the seventeenth century and refers in a joking way to the best method for polishing wood. A particularly British association lies in the old workshop tradition of playing tricks on new apprentices. In printing shops, one practice was to drop a tray of typefaces and make the unfortunate youngster spend hours putting them back in their order. Many practical jokes played on an apprentice's ignorance, and included sending him to fetch some elbow grease, a wild-goose chase in which the gullible youngster would be sent ever onward until he either caught on to the joke or gave up.

Fair play (noun)

Quintessentially British notion of sportsmanship and chivalry.

Shakespeare used both the phrases *fair play* and *foul play* in his works, and may well have coined both, thus giving us principles for behavior that have become legendary in the British character. Whatever precisely Shakespeare meant by them—his sense may have been closer to the idea of mere civilized observance and its opposite—today we interpret *fair play* to mean sportsmanship, playing by the rules with a certain nobility of spirit. There may well be leftover chivalric courtesy in the term, implying that there are underhand or

ignoble deeds or actions that
a gentleman simply doesn't
engage in. Children of a certain
period learned these rules at school
and, equally, through the rules of the
playground. In childhood fights, you didn't
attack someone from behind, when they
were on the ground, or fight two against
one. These were all unwritten rules which
were honored as much as the written rules of team games.

It is depressing now, against the background of that
tradition, to see the average level of behavior of highly paid
soccer players—tripping from behind, shirt-grabbing, and
elbowing, in a hyped-up atmosphere where almost everything
goes. There was a time, I seem to remember, when "the
beautiful game" really was more beautiful, when players
respected the spirit, the character, and the image of the game,
and understood the real meaning of fair play.

Flutter (verb)

An innocent little gamble by amateur Brits.

This is a lovely old word with a venerable history, meaning
to float gently up and down on the waves, or to move in the
air. At present, its popular sense of placing a small bet comes
from that charming British tradition that allows us to have
a few minor vices without guilt. Betting and gambling are of
course social evils, and the Protestant streak in British life,
dating from the Reformation, certainly does not approve of

that. However, the whole nation can guiltlessly turn out for the Grand National, the most exciting horse race on the calendar, and have a flutter, or place a wager. I like the word's suggestion of a slightly racing heartbeat, which expresses so nicely the amateurish pleasure of the whole moment. It is believed that the Queen herself, a keen horse enthusiast as well as owner, has a little flutter on the side. And if she doesn't, her mother in her time certainly did.

Googly (noun)

Cricket term originally meaning a challenging throw of the ball to an opponent.

The English language is full of phrases borrowed from cricket, such as "keep a straight bat" or "be completely stumped," or "on a sticky wicket." Often these have some moral or philosophical edge to them, associated with the traditionally upright image of the game. "It isn't cricket!" was once how a certain brand of Englishman protested against a less than honorable action. "Play up, play up, and play the game," went the inspiring refrain of the Victorian Sir Henry Newbolt's poem "Vitaï Lampada," about a young man learning endurance on the cricket field of his school, then going into the horrors of the First World War:

The river of death has brimmed its banks,
And England's far, and Honor a name,
But the voice of a schoolboy rallies the ranks—
"Play up! Play up! And play the game!"

Probably a good deal of this noble moralizing has been lost with the state of the modern game.

One nice term that survives in general use, and that defies translation, is the *googly*, a way of throwing the ball so that it lands in one direction and then bounces in another, thus confusing the batsman. The word now means any tricky challenge presented to an opponent or competitor. "I bowled him a real googly," one might say with delight.

Hair of the dog (that bit you) (noun phrase)

Dubious hangover cure consisting of a small amount of the same drink that led to the hangover.

Across the Queen's green and pleasant land on any Sunday morning, you can be sure that a good number of her loyal subjects are nursing a fierce headache after one pint or two too many the previous evening. British folk wisdom dictates that a shot of the drink that got you into this state—*a hair of the dog that bit you*—will supposedly clear your head in no time. The phrase is thought to come from the ancient medical principle that like cures like, according to which a dog bite would be healed by rubbing it with a burned hair of the offending dog.

Humbug! (exclamation)

*An exclamation of disgust used by Dickens's fictional character
Ebenezer Scrooge in* A Christmas Carol.

First recorded in the eighteenth century as a slang word
meaning hoax or jest, humbug has come to be associated
with a particular character in literature. Or should I say, "Bah!
Humbug!" Then everyone will know that I am quoting the most
famously unlikable hero of all time, namely, Charles Dickens's
Ebenezer Scrooge in A *Christmas Carol.*

We know that Scrooge hated Christmas and thought
it a waste of time, not to mention money. He despised the
merriment around him and was disinclined even to let his poor
overworked clerk, Bob Cratchit, have Christmas Day off with
his family.

To every suggestion of generosity, bonhomie, or kindness,
Scrooge's scowling riposte was "Bah! Humbug!" But then,
through some kind of miraculous intervention, involving

the ghosts of Christmas past, present, and future, he
underwent a conversion and became sensitive, kind, and
unable to pass a poor man in the street without offering to
help him. The phrase today is often uttered by the grumpy
and curmudgeonly.

"It" (noun)

A prudish reference to sex which is typically British. Part of a tradition of comic innuendo that goes back all the way to Chaucer and Shakespeare.

Of course, nobody knows what "it" is, but that's the whole point. The British, in their amusingly bashful way, can only ever refer to sex indirectly. Hence we see, often as stickers in the back window of cars, CLIMBERS DO IT ON MOUNTAINS or CAMPERS DO IT IN TENTS. The variations are endlessly creative. Such innuendo is a staple ingredient of British humor, riddled with puns, *double entendre,* and genially disguised "filth" and goes back all the way to Chaucer and Shakespeare.

Humphrey Lyttelton, erstwhile presenter of a popular radio show called *I'm Sorry, I Haven't a Clue*, invented an imaginary assistant called Samantha and opened the show every week with some scandalously ambiguous comment, such as: "Samantha once trained opera singers—having seen what she did to the baritone, the director is keen to see what she might do for a tenor."

The special quality of innuendo, of course, is to make the statement in all innocence, so the device is frequently used where children can happily take one meaning, while adults will see the sexual reference. *Balloons, jugs, melons, buns, beaver, muff, poker, tool, staff, snake, sword*—all these can figure in innuendo as indirect references to parts of the body. The whole sense and enjoyment is in the ambiguity of interpretation. In a classic example of this, academics are still arguing over whether or not Shakespeare's "Sonnet 52," written for his beloved young lord, is pure sexual innuendo from beginning to end: "So am I as the rich, whose blessed key/Can bring him to his sweet up-locked treasure."

Today there is a tendency in movie and drama production to make Shakespeare's sexual references more explicit, which may well reflect how his lines were played in his own time. This is a sign of modern times and tastes, but in the case of Jane Austen and more modest classical authors, can result in a loss of the subtlety and wit of the original.

Knuckle down (verb)

To begin working or studying hard, but without complaining (which would be un-British).

Knuckling down strikes me as a very British characteristic, in the sense of accepting difficulties that arise and just getting on with things. It is all the more surprising that its origin is the humble game of marbles, and comes from the rule that you must keep your knuckle down where your marble has just been. From that rule, to knuckle down had the eighteenth-century dictionary sense of "to stoop, bend, yield, comply with, or submit to." Of course, the unspoken rule in British behavior is to accept without complaint, and so we have made this a positive virtue, applying oneself to the task as needed. This is very different from *knuckle under*, which has retained the original meaning of connoting submissiveness, but comes from American usage.

Manners makyth man (expression)

The Brits are famous for observing good manners at all costs and judging others by theirs.

This was the motto of the famous medieval churchman and lawman, William of Wykeham (1320–1404), who founded Winchester College and New College, Oxford, and gave both these institutions the same motto to guide their work of education. We can imagine that he must have thought himself the living proof of his wisdom, as he was born to a humble family and rose through his own talents (and good manners, one supposes) to be Lord Privy Seal and Lord Chancellor.

The principle that the aims of education should include good manners was still alive and well in 1947, when the Advisory Report on Secondary Education in Scotland affirmed that "the good school is to be assessed not by any tale of examination successes, however impressive, but by the extent to which it has filled the years of youth with security, graciousness, and ordered freedom."

That word *graciousness* is not one that springs to mind these days, when we observe the public behavior of schoolchildren. For example, with more and more pupils now boarding free buses in London, their noise and rowdiness increasingly alarms other passengers.

Mind your Ps and Qs (expression)

*A gentle admonition, usually to children, to mind their manners, perhaps as they are about to go to tea with a **maiden aunt**.*

There are a dozen suggestions for the derivation of this saying, ranging from the instructions of a French dancing master to mind your feet and wigs (*pieds et queues*), to advice for apprentice printers not to mix up metal type, a tavern keeper's traditional method of chalking up *pints and quarts* drunk by their clients, or quite simply a shortened corruption of *pleases and thank-yous.*

We all have our favorite explanation, mine being the printer's guard against confusion over the similar and reversible shape of Ps and Qs. Some have argued that these are not such common letters as Bs and Ds which are also reversible, therefore why not mind your Bs and Ds? But this misses the whole point that, in the font tray, Ps and Qs are actually side by side.

More tea, vicar? (expression)

A comic British phrase that associates the kindly vicar with all kinds of subjects that are rude, namely sex.

"More tea, vicar?" For most British people, if someone suddenly comes out with that line, it will be thought funny, or at least raise a smile. We may ask, what is funny about it? But as soon as we ask, it stops being funny. This is because our sense of humor has less to do with what is said, and more to do with our attitude toward life in general. And as a rule, the more important the topic, the more likely we are to be humorous about it. Vicars are pillars of society, and on those grounds alone they are intrinsically funny. In situation comedy, male vicars are stock characters, usually gentle, fussy individuals with good manners and intentions. They tend not to see or hear unpleasant things.

Nobody really knows any more where the line came from, but it can be imagined in the setting of a visit to a local parishioner for tea—a small event reflecting social life in a village. Something has occurred to upset the neat order of the household. It is likely to be something quite vulgar. So the lady of the house feels the need to cover up and preserve the delicacy of the moment: "More tea, vicar?" Vicars and vulgarity—the two extremes produce the spark, and in the process, we are really laughing at ourselves and at the things we hold dear.

Muck/mucky (noun, adjective)

*Dirt or filth of any kind. Also means manure when referring
to farming.*

For people doing serious things with the land, whether farming
or mining, *muck* is a serious word. Farmers spread it, miners
pile it high. Equally, nothing could be more serious than the
classic image of the feet-on-the-ground Yorkshire businessman
uttering the phrase, "Where there's muck, there's brass." This is
not a new idea, nor even an exclusively northern one, as shown
by the British proverb, "Muck and money go together," a saying
that goes back at least three hundred years.

In the English world at large, though, muck has no value,
just the opposite. Muck is basically dirt. In the past, the form
muck-a-muck or *muckety-muck* was used as a taunting name
for someone of airs and self-importance, perhaps because the
appealingly blunt sound of the word could bring anyone down
a peg. It is a four-letter word, after all, with kinship to the Old
Norse term, *myki*, meaning "dung." From dirt in a physical
sense, it has also come to mean *filth*, that is, morally dubious
entertainment.

Muck and *mucky* appear in many different sayings, (*muck
about, muck in, muck around, muck up*) as well as songs and
phrases. Though widely used throughout England, the words
continue to have a northern ring to them, and I especially like
the use in Stan Kelly's 1960s song, "The Liverpool Lullaby,"
recorded in an inimitable accent by Cilla Black:

Oh you are a mucky kid,
Dirty as a dustbin lid.
When he hears the things you did,
You'll gerra belt from your Dad.

On the pull (expression)

Out looking for a sexual partner, a term often used when going out to
a pub or club.

One of those British terms that seems to baffle Americans,
though the basic practice itself must be familiar. It is a truth
universally acknowledged that single men and women are
constantly in search of the ideal partner and therefore part
of the social game is to go out hunting. But unlike in other
centuries, when brute force or wealth alone brought about
success in this area, the modern hunt takes place in the absurd
hope that somehow your personality will display irresistible
magnetic properties, preferably for someone so attractive that
they would normally never look at you. Thus, to be *on the pull*
is to live in a continuing state of self-delusion and unfounded
optimism.

There are no statistics to back this up, but anecdotally it
does seem that ninety-nine percent of young people on the
pull go home alone at the end of an evening.

Queue (noun, verb)

A line of people waiting patiently for a service or event, always conducted in an orderly fashion.

The queue is part of the fabric of British society, yet it isn't really clear why English people form an orderly queue for almost every occasion, while those on the **Continent** do not. But as we have already seen, the Continent is "a foreign country: They do things differently there." Perhaps the explanation is that we display a mixture of diffidence and fairness, both profoundly English qualities, in our attitude to queuing. On the one hand, we hate to push ourselves forward—for that would be making ourselves conspicuous, and therefore very **un-English**—and on the other hand, we recognize the right of those who came first to claim their place.

The corollary to the queuing theory is that *queue jumpers* are never challenged, but only silently regarded with the contempt they deserve.

Quite (adverb)

Versatile adverb that, depending on context, may mean one is being very modest or very definite.

Along with rather, quite is one of those qualifying words that expresses typically English reservation and unwillingness to overstate anything, or, as our enemies might add, to say anything very clearly at all. I am quite sure they are wrong, however, as even the word *quite*, as here exemplified, can have a gently, modestly, undramatically, reinforcing value as well. When an Englishman is quite sure, you can be certain he is very sure.

Right of way (noun)

The privilege to pass over another person's land, prized by ramblers.

The British do get bees in their bonnets about some things, and the rights of the individual are high on that list. But rather than the massive street demonstrations held on the **Continent**, the British way is to go quietly about protecting their rights through small, but effective, gestures. Almost emblematic of the small man's struggle against oppression, is the issue of rights of way, or public footpaths. Many of these are centuries old and, without vigilance, can fall into disuse or become blocked by landowners. The Ramblers Association, with some 140,000 members, campaigns for the right of walkers to access land and coast, and in 2000 its efforts were crowned with some success in establishing a *right to roam*.

Rigmarole (noun)

A complicated, petty set of procedures, such as those set by government departments.

As we see above, the British don't care much for bureaucracy, and are quick to condemn lengthy and complicated procedures, any of which may be termed a *rigmarole*. The utter rigmarole involved in claiming social service benefits, for instance, is said to explain why millions of pounds of rightful payments are left unclaimed every year.

The origins of this word go back hundreds of years, revealing that the problem is nothing new. It appears to have arisen from the existence of a medieval game called "Ragman," possibly named for a French character known as *Ragemon*. This was a game for educated and literate clerks, and played with a long scroll full of written descriptions of personalities. Each section was marked off with a hanging string or ribbon, and the scroll was rolled up. The players then took turns choosing a string, unrolling the scroll, and reading out the description that presumably, by default, was taken to apply to themselves, to the merriment of all.

When, in 1291, the defeated Scottish nobles signed promises of loyalty to King Edward I (so-called Hammer of the Scots), all their deeds and seals were joined in a huge roll, forty feet long, delivered to the king in London. As the whole thing bore a resemblance to the scroll of the old game, it became familiarly known as the *Ragman Roll*. Over time, and through various changes, this has come down to us as *rigmarole*, meaning any rambling and drawn-out procedure or implausibly complicated explanation.

Soppy (adjective)

Weak or overly sentimental characteristics that are disdained by the Brits.

The British have so many condemnatory words for the weak and ineffectual that you have to conclude our self-image is that of a people who are tough, resistant, and able to adapt to hardship. And that is exactly how we see ourselves.

When Mrs. Thatcher famously said to a minister, "Don't be so wet!" she struck a chord with the public. Wet means soppy, which means lacking resolution or the capacity to make difficult decisions. In an interesting nuance, *soppy* also means soft in relationships, showing one's feelings too much, which of course is a very **un-English** thing to do.

Another popular phrase is *big girl's blouse*, meaning a weak and ineffectual man. No one seems to know where this comes from, but it has a bluff, northern sound to it, and may have come into more common use from a 1960s TV series about life in the north of England. It could be simply an extension of the phrase "Big girl!" said scornfully of a man lacking masculine qualities. Whatever its origin, it does conjure up wonderfully a kind of flappy, floppy image, the very opposite of a tough, upstanding male.

Sorry (exclamation)

A characteristically self-effacing phrase often used as a passive-aggressive substitute for a direct accusation.

As we have seen time and time again, English is a minefield for the nonnative speaker, especially in the case of phrases and expressions that mean just the opposite of what they appear to say. For instance, Elton John may have sung that "Sorry seems to be the hardest word," but for most English people, the opposite is true. The word *sorry* is heard constantly as a mollifying disguise for grievance, in situations where you would normally expect the speaker to express anger or upset. Look out for: "I'm sorry, but there seems to be a fly in my soup," or "I'm sorry, but I've been waiting for over an hour to be served."

It is quite plain that, here, the speakers are not apologizing, as such; they simply want to make clear that an embarrassing situation has arisen. As the English hate public embarrassment of any kind, however, we bend over backward to avoid making any direct accusation. So next time someone stands on your foot in a London crowd, you know exactly what to say: "Sorry!"

Spend a penny (verb)

A rather charming phrase meaning to visit the bathroom.

Here's a challenge for an American visitor to England. You ask a waiter for directions to the restroom, which is your polite way of saying you want to relieve yourself, and the waiter stares blankly. What now?

Well, there are many euphemistic phrases for this most basic of human needs, but many of them are meant for an informal setting and therefore not suitable for your restaurant or café waiter. Let's get through the unsuitable ones first. To *spend a penny* comes from the old practice, literally, of having to put a penny in the door of a public bathroom to use it. "To see a man about a dog" is an informal phrase that appears to go back to the mid-nineteenth century and in its earlier sense meant to go and visit a woman sexually. In a creative variant, I recently heard someone say, "I need to see a cossack about a borzoi." These days, "to pass water" or "to have a pee/slash" are far too direct to be used in polite company.

But, as you are in a bit of a hurry, we had better get to the point. You should ask your waiter, "Where is the ladies/gents, please?" Or you can use the upper classes' hygienic euphemism, "Where can I wash my hands?"

Loo is a middle to upper class euphemism for lavatory, and though rather familiar, not especially offensive to use. It derives from Waterloo, the verbal

connection being obvious if not any other. The only association I know between the 1815 Battle of Waterloo and lavatories stems from the Duke of Wellington being asked by a young officer's mother what best advice he could give her son starting on a military career.

The duke is supposed to have uttered the unforgettable reply of "Never miss an opportunity to pass water."

Stiff upper lip (noun phrase)

Displaying fortitude in the face of adversity, as opposed to a trembling of the upper lip, which to a Brit is an unforgivable sign of weakness.

Keeping a stiff upper lip denotes a quintessentially British outlook on life that gives us several valuable clues as to the British character. It describes a very British way of reacting to life's little ups and downs: uncomplaining stoicism and composure under pressure.

In many ways, it can be seen as an extension of the complicated social etiquette that British people hold so dear. The British will go to great lengths to keep up appearances and not draw attention to themselves, either by keeping quiet and soldiering on in the face of adversity, or by remaining polite, patient, and respectful, even when provoked.

Sweet Fanny Adams (noun phrase)

*A euphemism for **** all.*

This saying, unlike many, has a clear historical source, though
its path to its current meaning of absolutely nothing has been
rather circuitous. Poor Fanny Adams was the child victim of
a murderer, her dismembered corpse was found in August of
1867 in the town of Alton, England. (Her tombstone can still be
seen there.) Much public outrage and discussion surrounded
the arrest and execution of her murderer and the child herself
became widely known as Sweet Fanny Adams because of her
age and innocence.

Around the same time, the Royal Navy introduced tinned
meat rations, which sailors disliked and referred to as *Sweet
Fanny Adams* in a grisly association with the murder. As such,
the expression spread into wider use as meaning something
of little or no value, and was commonly shortened to *Sweet FA*.
In modern usage the phrase has become crossed with another,
more impolite *FA*, which also means "absolutely nothing."
Australian W. H. Downing recorded this latter use in his 1919
publication *Digger Dialects*.

Turned out nice again (expression)

A half-hearted greeting.

It is commonly acknowledged (see **dog's life**) that walking
around in public with a dog allows one to be quite **un-English**
and talk to people we have not been introduced to. But what
recourse is available in the event that we haven't got a dog? At

any moment we may pass a neighbor in the street, or someone
we recognize even if we can't quite remember their name or
who they are. One cannot simply stare at the sidewalk and it
would be unforgivably rude to say nothing, so what can we say
that will safely mean absolutely nothing? We must talk about
the weather. "Turned out nice again," we say cheerfully as we
stride on. And so the danger is past.

And what was the danger, exactly? The danger was that
the person might just be one of those who, despite all the
rules, wants to draw you into conversation and talk endlessly
about their latest woes, or worse, ask you searching personal
questions about your life, hopes, and anxieties.

Un-English (adjective)

Any behavior that contradicts the rules of good manners and customs.

Another book would be needed to list all that is un-English,
for it seems we are defined as much by what we wouldn't
dream of doing, as by what we actually do. Such inhibition
gives us kinship with other cultures, like the Japanese, where
correctness rules. British sense and sensibility are renowned,
and yet many of our fellow-Europeans see our behavior, dress,
and eating habits as uncouth. But it is not un-English to be
badly dressed, or rowdy in conversation, or eat junk food.
Our rules are supposed to govern other things: emotions,
confidences, openness, familiarity, and privacy.

With respect (adverbial phrase)

Used as a polite formula to imply disagreement.

Another of those confusing little British expressions which, in fact, means exactly the opposite of the words used. (See **Don't mind me!**)

Yuck! (exclamation)

A very English expression used to indicate disgust.

Perhaps the most common general expression of distaste or disgust among English children. It appears in Samuel Johnson's *Dictionary of the English Language* as a noun meaning "itch," and in this sense comes from the Middle English *yicche*.
I like its straightforward, unequivocal sound, and the fact that it has miraculously not become an obscenity over the centuries, like so many other four-letter words.

XXXX-words (noun)

Rude or censored words that cannot be mentioned within the pages of this book for fear of causing offense.

In 1965, for the first time ever, critic Kenneth Tynan used a sexual four-letter word on TV and motions of censure were signed by over a hundred members of Parliament. The BBC had to issue a formal apology. Eleven years later, suspensions followed the Sex Pistols' swearing on ITV's *Today* show. These days, with reality TV taking over, controls are nearly impossible and the boundaries of propriety are moving. It's interesting, then, to note that today's XXXX-words are not so much sexual as social. In recent weeks, broadcasters have been scolded for uttering terms like *pikey*, *chav*, and **toff** in derogatory contexts referring to social categories. Historically, *pikeys* were turnpike travelers of gypsy background long seen as fringe people. *Chav* is a Romany word meaning simply "lad," but has recently become associated with a brand of surly youth culture.

Debating the use of these terms, along with jibes such as *pleb* and *prol*—which refer to plebeian and proletarian, respectively—some see a resurgence of social tension in Britain. Others say, quite simply, that political correctness has gone too far. "Ban pikey," wrote Des Kelly in the *Daily Mail*, "and you might as well outlaw chav, townie, trailer trash, Hooray Henry, goth, Sloane, tinker, and many more fairly innocuous labels."

Word Finder

Sources

Andrews, R., Brown, J., Humphreys, R., and Lee, P., *The Rough Guide to England* (Rough Guides; UK, 2008)

Austen, Jane, *Northanger Abbey* (John Murray; London, 1817)

Barone, James, "Comparing apples and oranges: a randomised prospective study" (British Medical Journal; 2000, December 23; 321 (7276): 1569–1570)

Brewer, E. Cobham, *Dictionary of Phrase and Fable* (Henry Altemus; Philadelphia, 1898)

Bryson, Bill, *Mother Tongue: The English Language* (Penguin; UK, 1999)

Chaucer, Geoffrey, *The Riverside Chaucer* (Oxford University Press; Oxford, 2008)

Fowler H.W. and Fowler F.G., *The King's English* (Clarendon Press; Oxford, 1908)

Fox, Adam, *Oral and Literate Culture in England* (Oxford University Press; Oxford, 2000)

Fox, Kate, *Watching the English: The Hidden Rules of English Behaviour,* (Hodder and Stoughton; UK, 2005)

Gower, John, *Confessio Amantis* 1393 (The Echo Library; UK, 2007)

Harrington, J., Palethorpe, S., and Watson, C., "Does the Queen speak the Queen's English?" (Nature; 2000, December 21; 408, 927–928)

Jerome, Jerome K., *Three Men in a Boat* (J.W. Arrowsmith; UK, 1889)

Jonson, Ben, *Timber: or, Discoveries* (1641), in *The Works of Ben Jonson,* ed. C. H. Herford and Percy Simpson (11 vols., Oxford, 1925-52, viii. 625)

Johnson, Samuel, *Dr. Johnson's Dictionary* (Penguin Classics; UK, 2005)

Kelly, Stan, "The Liverpool Lullaby" (song) recorded by Cilla Black,1969

Kipling, Rudyard, *The Complete Verse* (Kyle Cathie; London, revised edition 2006)

Newbolt, Henry, *Collected Poems of Henry Newbolt* (Thomas Nelson & Sons; UK, 1907)

Pepys, Samuel, *The Diaries of Samuel Pepys—A Selection* (Penguin Classics; UK, 2003)

Pliny the Elder, *Natural History* (Penguin Classics; UK, reprint edition 2004)

Quinion, Michael, www.worldwidewords.org (ISSUE 456; 27 August 2005)

Shakespeare, William, *The Complete Works of William Shakespeare* (Wordsworth Editions Ltd; UK, new edition 1996)

Sheldrake, Rupert, *Seven Experiments that Could Change the World* (Riverhead Books; USA, 1996)

Shaw, Bernard, *Pygmalion* (Brentano; New York, 1916)

Sheridan, Richard, *The Rivals* (Nick Hern Books; UK, new edition 1994)

Sterne, Laurence, *The Life and Opinions of Tristram Shandy, Gentleman* (Penguin; UK, 1998)

Wilde, Oscar, *The Complete Works of Oscar Wilde* (Collins; UK, new edition 2003)

Wilson Thomas, *Art of Rhetorique,* 1553 (Benediction Classics; Oxford, 2007)